A Trainer's Guide

to

Caring for Children in School-Age Programs

Derry G. Koralek

Debra D. Foulks

Cover design by

Jennifer Barrett O'Connell

TEACHING STRATEGIES INC.

P.O. Box 42243

Washington, DC 20015

Published by

Teaching Strategies, Inc.
P.O. Box 42243
Washington, DC 20015

Distributed by

Gryphon House, Inc.
P.O. Box 207
Beltsville, MD 20704-0207

ISBN: 1-879537-16-8

Library of Congress Catalog Card Number: 95-060882

Acknowledgments

Caring for Children in School-Age Programs and this *Trainer's Guide* are based on materials originally developed by Teaching Strategies, Inc., for the U.S. Army Child and Youth Services. We would like to acknowledge two individuals who contributed to the development process. First, we want to thank M.-A. Lucas, Chief of Army Child and Youth Services, who recognized the important role school-age programs play in the lives of children and initiated the development of this training program. Next, we express our gratitude to Dr. Victoria Moss, Program Manager, Supplemental Programs and Services, Department of the Army, who guided the development of the training modules and this *Trainer's Guide*. Her constructive and helpful suggestions greatly improved this publication.

Contents

Introduction

A wide variety of organizations operate school-age programs for the out-of-school hours of children in kindergarten through sixth grade. Typically, children participate in these programs for an hour or more before school, for several hours after school, and full-time during vacation periods. In effective, high-quality school-age programs, this time is used to introduce children to new topics and ideas, to involve them in sports and recreational activities, and to encourage interests and skills children will carry into adulthood. Such programs rely on the skills and knowledge of school-age staff who plan, guide, and facilitate children's participation.

Sound staff training is an essential factor in achieving a high-quality school-age program. *Caring for Children in School-Age Programs* offers comprehensive, performance-based training. Because the program is self-instructional, staff can use it at their own pace, as time permits. This approach allows for staff autonomy in completing the training. But that autonomy also means trainers must play a very active role in advising staff during the training and in tracking their progress. The trainer's central role is to provide feedback and support and to make judgments about the appropriateness of a staff member's responses in the Learning Activities. Trainers also observe and model appropriate practices in school-age programs and assess the knowledge and competence staff have gained from the training.

This *Trainer's Guide* has four chapters and seven appendices. Chapter I, An Overview of *Caring for Children in School-Age Programs*, describes the content, format, and training approach. The chapter also discusses how to offer training based on adult learning principles; describes the professional development and program improvement efforts in the field of school-age care; and offers suggestions for making training count.

Chapter II, Overseeing the Training Program, provides an overview of the trainer's role in introducing the training program, completing the Orientation, and working through a module. It also discusses providing feedback, describes what staff and trainers do to complete each module, and offers suggested strategies for extending learning.

Chapter III, Leading Group Training Sessions, is targeted to trainers who will implement the training through settings such as workshops, seminars, or college courses. It describes training techniques, logistics, strategies for encouraging active participation, and methods for evaluating training. A sample training outline is provided for Module 10, Guidance.

Chapter IV, Assessing Each Staff Member's Progress, explains the assessment process and includes Knowledge and Competency Assessments for the modules.

The appendices include a planning form for group training sessions, the Knowledge Assessment answer sheets, observation forms for the Competency Assessments, tracking forms, a training record, a certificate of completion, and a list of publishers and distributors of the resources on school-age programming described in the Orientation to *Caring for Children in School-Age Programs*.

I. An Overview of *Caring for Children in School-Age Programs*

I. An Overview of *Caring for Children in School-Age Programs*

This chapter describes:

- the content and format of the training program;

- the training approach;

- understanding how adults learn;

- professional development and program improvement efforts in the field of school-age care; and

- making training count.

The Content and Format of the Training Program

Caring for Children in School-Age Programs is fourth in Teaching Strategies' series of competency-based training programs for adults who care for children in centers and family child care homes. It is designed to help school-age staff gain the skills needed to plan and implement a developmentally appropriate program for children ages 5 through 12. The training program is comprehensive, covering the key knowledge and skills needed by staff working in school-age programs. The training is competency-based, combining a self-instructional approach with support and feedback from a trainer. Staff complete Learning Activities while working with the children in the program. Then, they discuss their growing skills and knowledge with their trainer. Assessment completes the training cycle for each module. Both Knowledge and Competency Assessments are provided so staff can confirm their understanding of the concepts presented and demonstrate their skills while on the job.

The Content Addressed in *Caring for Children In School-Age Programs*

As with the other volumes in the *Caring for . . .* series, this training program is organized according to the 13 functional areas covered by the Child Development Associate (CDA) Competency Standards as defined by The Council for Early Childhood Professional Recognition in Washington, DC. Each module addresses a specific functional area: Safe, Healthy, Program Environment (titled Learning Environment for CDA), Physical, Cognitive, Communication, Creative, Self, Social, Guidance, Families, Program Management, and Professionalism. (See the Orientation in *Caring for Children in School-Age Programs* for definitions of each functional area.)

Children are continually learning and developing. Consequently, everything children do at a school-age program has the potential for being a positive experience that enhances their growth and development. *Caring for Children in School-Age Programs* provides many examples of how a school-age program can complement rather than duplicate children's school experiences and allow children to explore special interests and talents.

School-age programs typically enroll a wide age range of children, from those entering the primary grades to those on the verge of adolescence. It is extremely challenging to provide a program that meets the needs of all children as they move from early childhood, to middle childhood, to preadolescence, to the teen years. To help staff understand how children's skills and needs vary during these years, *Caring for Children in School-Age Programs* focuses on the developmental characteristics of three age groups: 5 to 7 years, 8 to 10 years, and 11 to 12 years. A number of key skills and concepts are repeated and reinforced throughout the modules. These include the following:

- **Competent school-age staff conduct systematic, objective observations.** Observations allow staff to learn about each child, measure children's progress, and evaluate program effectiveness. Information gathered through regular, systematic observations help staff learn about each child's needs, skills, and interests. This information is used in planning for the group and to individualize the program.

- **Effective school-age programs offer balance.** Staff create interest areas and plan activities that offer active and quiet experiences, take place indoors and outdoors, and involve individuals as well as small and large groups. Some activities are planned and introduced by staff and some are initiated by children. Children can spend time in same-age and multi-age groupings, participate in cooperative and competitive ways, and use socio-emotional, physical, and cognitive skills.

- **School-age children need many opportunities to make choices.** Children can choose what they want to do and with whom. For example, children lead group meetings, participate in routines, and choose from multiple activity options each day. Staff establish and stock interest areas according to children's skills and interests. They use surveys and other techniques to keep up with children's changing interests. In addition, the daily schedule provides long blocks of time when children can plan and carry out their ideas.

- **The primary role of school-age staff is to facilitate children's involvement in the program.** Staff set up an interesting and challenging environment, provide materials, and plan activities that reflect children's needs, skills, and interests. Staff respond to children's requests for assistance in carrying out their plans and encourage children to develop and use new skills.

- **Children are part of a community within the program and in the larger world beyond.** School-age programs encourage children to be a part of both communities. Staff provide many opportunities for children to be meaningfully involved in program planning and operations. They coordinate with other agencies and youth programs to involve children in the larger community so children can develop and use their skills and interests.

To reinforce the content presented in the training program, there are numerous examples of children and staff actively involved in high-quality school-age programs. The programs depicted in these examples have sufficient indoor and outdoor space, meet recommended child-adult ratios, provide well-stocked interest areas, and offer a balance of activities that respond to the skills and interests of the children enrolled. The human interactions in the examples demonstrate appropriate staff practices that facilitate children's growth and learning. Some high-quality school-age programs do not operate in the "ideal" environments described in these examples, perhaps because the space and financial resources dedicated to the program are insufficient. Programs may operate in inadequate space, playgrounds may be unsafe or located at a distance from the program, and materials and equipment may be in disrepair or inappropriate for the ages and interests of the children enrolled. If this is true of the school-age programs with which you work, *Caring for Children in School-Age Programs* can serve as both a tool for increasing staff competence and as support for requesting additional space and funding.

The Format of the Training Program

The training program consists of a two-volume set for staff and this *Trainer's Guide*. Volume I includes the Orientation and Modules 1 through 6; Volume II includes Modules 7 through 13. Each module begins with an Overview to the topic which is followed by five to six Learning Activities to be completed by staff as they work with children.

The *Trainer's Guide* provides suggestions for overseeing the program, offering feedback, leading group training, and assessing competence. In addition, this guide provides Knowledge and Competency Assessments, answer sheets, planning and tracking forms, and other information to help trainers in their role.

Caring for Children in School-Age Programs

For Staff:

For Trainers:

Contents

Overseeing the Program

Offering Feedback

Leading Group Training

Assessing Competence

> **Knowledge Assessments**

> **Competency Assessments**

Planning and Tracking

Forms

The Training Approach

The training approach used in *Caring for Children in School-Age Programs* combines self-instruction with support and feedback from a trainer. Staff begin by completing the Orientation, a summary of the training content and process. Next, each staff member meets with the trainer to develop an Individual Training Plan, an outline of the order in which the staff member plans to work on the modules. To complete each module, staff read the Overview, complete a Pre-Training Assessment of their skills, and do five to six Learning Activities. The Learning Activities include several pages of text and Applying Your Knowledge, an opportunity for staff members to build skills related to the topic.

The role of trainers begins by introducing the program to staff. Throughout the training process, trainers observe staff as they work with children and provide feedback and support during one-on-one and group training sessions. They address individual learning styles by offering additional resources and approaches and by suggesting strategies for extending learning for staff who want to enhance their professional development. As staff complete each module, the trainer assesses their knowledge and competence and tracks their progress. Chapter II, Overseeing the Training Program, provides a more detailed description of what staff and trainers do during the training.

Understanding How Adults Learn

Caring for Children in School-Age Programs was developed to meet the unique characteristics and training needs of school-age staff and programs. The training materials can be used by new or experienced staff to increase their knowledge and understanding of school-age children and appropriate programming for out-of-school hours and to build skills in planning and implementing quality school-age programs. The self-instructional, competency-based approach allows staff to apply their learning immediately while working with children. As a result, staff can see how their professional development affects children and contributes to overall program improvement efforts. Perhaps the most important feature of the training program is the way it reflects an understanding of how adults learn.

Adult learning principles were taken into account in the design and implementation of *Caring for Children in School-Age Programs*. The training program is used on the job as part of the ongoing work of school-age staff. It respects the work and life experiences of staff by acknowledging and building on what they already know. Staff actively participate in their own individualized training and receive extensive feedback from trainers. And the training emphasizes hands-on learning through activities completed as staff work with children.

Meeting the unique needs of adult learners such as school-age staff can be very challenging. Most adults are self-directed and want to be responsible for their own learning. How much they get out of training depends on how important the content is to them, how much effort they put into the learning process, and whether they integrate and use what they learn. Trainers need to consider what motivates adults to learn and how principles of adult learning theory can be applied to training.

What Motivates Adults to Learn?

For most adults, motivation for learning is closely related to whether there is an immediate use for the information and skills being addressed. They want to know what they will be learning so they can determine whether it is useful. This training program defines clear objectives in the Self-Assessment, the Pre-Training Assessments, and at the beginning of each Learning Activity, so staff can clearly see what they will be learning and how it relates to school-age care.

Adults view job-related learning as a means to an end, not an end in itself. They are motivated to participate in training that allows them to develop or improve specific job-related skills. The Learning Activities in *Caring for Children in School-Age Programs* address this motivator because they are completed on the job.

Time is a limited and valuable investment for working adults. They have more positive attitudes towards training when they believe the time invested is well-spent. The knowledge and skills gained through this training program will make staff more effective in their work with children. Trainers can reinforce this motivator by pointing out to staff how children are benefiting from their increased skills and knowledge.

Strong secondary factors relating to an adult's motivation to learn are to build their self-esteem and to increase their enjoyment of work. This training program acknowledges and builds on what staff already know. It includes opportunities for staff to feel successful and competent as they complete Learning Activities, modules, and the assessment process. Staff who know they are competent tend to enjoy their work and want to continue learning.

According to many studies, motivation increases with recognition for achievements, respect for the individual as a person, and participation in planning and decision making. The assessment process in *Caring for Children in School-Age Programs* provides recognition for accomplishments, and the self-paced, individualized approach demonstrates respect for each person's unique training needs. There are many opportunities for staff to plan and make decisions about their learning. For example, staff decide the order in which to complete the modules, when they are ready to be assessed, which child to observe for a Learning Activity, and what activity to plan, implement, and evaluate.

Adults are Motivated to Learn When They Can:

Immediately apply skills and knowledge.

Develop or improve specific skills.

See that their time is well-spent.

Increase self-esteem and pleasure.

Be recognized for their achievements.

Feel respected.

Participate in planning and decision making.

How Can Trainers Apply the Principles of Adult Learning Theory?

Adults bring a wealth of previous experiences to training. They find training more meaningful when their life experiences are recognized and they can relate the content to their own lives. For example, the Overview of each module includes an opportunity for staff to relate the content to their own lives and the Pre-Training Assessments allow them to rate their own skills.

Adults need opportunities to integrate new ideas with what they already know so they can use the new information. Training should provide opportunities to make interpretations and draw conclusions. The Learning Activities frequently encourage staff to reflect on their learning by answering questions about why they planned a specific activity, how children reacted, what they might do differently in the future, or how they can build on what they learned through the experience.

Adults acquire information that is conceptually new more slowly than information that relates to something they already know. The self-paced nature of this training program allows enough time for staff to learn and apply new concepts. In addition, because some Learning Activities build on previous ones, new concepts are repeated and reinforced.

Adults tend to acquire information even more slowly when it conflicts with what they already know, because it forces them to re-evaluate old knowledge. The trainer's feedback conferences with staff can serve as opportunities to discuss and evaluate new knowledge.

Adults tend to take errors personally and some find it difficult to take risks. This training program encourages reflection, critical thinking, and skill development rather than focusing on "right" or "wrong" answers. When answer sheets are provided, staff are encouraged to use them as a guide because there can be many possible correct responses.

Adults perceive their own experiences as unique and private. They are not always comfortable or willing to share these experiences with others. Each staff member receives a copy of *Caring for Children in School-Age Programs,* which can serve as a personal journal of that individual's professional development. Trainers need to respect a staff member's privacy while offering support and encouragement.

According to extensive research, adults learn best through a hands-on approach that actively involves them in the learning process. Edgar Dale explains this theory schematically in his "Cone of Experience," which appears on the next page.

Edgar Dale's Cone of Experience [*]

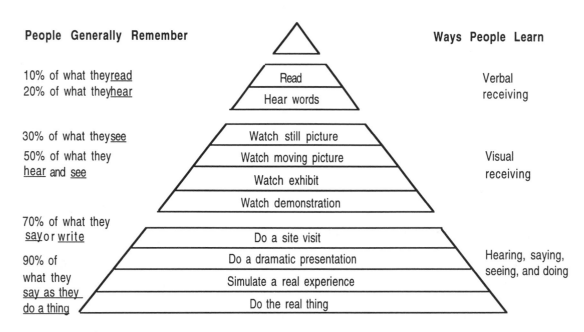

The Learning Activities in *Caring for Children in School-Age Programs* are indeed hands-on as they ask staff to "do the real thing." In addition to providing feedback after staff have completed Learning Activities, trainers can plan their schedules to include time to observe staff carrying out the activities.

---

[*] Based on Edgar Dale, *Audiovisual Methods in Teaching*; 3rd ed. (New York: Holt, Rinehart and Winston, 1969), p. 107.

Applying the Principles of Adult Learning

Principles of Adult Learning	What Trainers Can Do
Adults bring a wealth of experiences to training.	Use the Overview and Pre-Training Assessments to acknowledge what staff already know.
Adults need to integrate what they already know with new information.	Encourage staff to reflect on their own learning.
Adults need extra time to understand new information that doesn't relate to what they already know.	Respect the self-paced training approach so staff can take as much time as they need to internalize new information.
Adults need even more time to integrate information that conflicts with what they already know.	Use feedback conferences to discuss and evaluate "new" and "old" knowledge.
Adults tend to take errors personally and some have difficulty taking risks.	Emphasize reflection and critical thinking rather than "right" or "wrong" answers.
Adults perceive their own experiences as unique and private.	Provide individual copies of training materials and respect each person's privacy while offering support and encouragement.
Adults learn best through a hands-on approach.	Observe staff carrying out the Learning Activities.

Professional Development and Program Improvement Efforts in the Field of School-Age Care

Program directors, staff, trainers, and researchers in the field of school-age care are working together through the National School-Age Care Alliance (NSACA) to create professional development opportunities for school-age staff, including a national credential that will be recognized as formal acknowledgment of an individual's competence. At the same time, these leaders are establishing standards for quality and a national accreditation system for school-age programs. *Caring for Children in School-Age Programs* supports both of these important efforts.

As noted earlier, the Child Development Associate (CDA) functional areas serve as the framework for the modules in *Caring for Children in School-Age Programs;* however, the CDA competency standards do not address school-age care. As a result, a group consensus process known as a "Delphi" was used to define the staff competencies to be addressed in the modules. The Delphi involved experts in the field of school-age care from military and civilian programs. The experts were balanced in geography and gender and represented the perspectives of parents, practitioners, and specialists with expertise in CDA, child development, school-age care, recreation, and youth services. Ten of the Delphi experts were board members of the National School-Age Care Alliance (NSACA).

The questionnaire used in the first round of the Delphi asked participants to provide five responses to each of 13 open-ended questions corresponding to the CDA functional areas. For example, participants were asked, "What are the most important competencies school-age program staff need to operate a **safe** program?" In two subsequent rounds the participants reviewed the responses of other experts, commented if desired, reflected on their own choices, then provided the final top ten rankings for each question.

The final Delphi rankings were used to define the competencies for the training program. In addition, to ensure that content fully addressed the skills and knowledge staff need to operate high quality school-age programs, the authors reviewed a number of other sources of standards for school-age programs including:

- *Assessing School-Age Child Care Quality (ASQ),* from the Wellesley School-Age Child Care Project;

- *Standards for Quality School-Age Child Care,* from the National Association of Elementary School Principals in collaboration with the Wellesley School-Age Child Care Project; and

- *Developmentally Appropriate Practice in School-Age Child Care Programs* and *Quality Criteria for School-Age Child Care Programs*, from Project Home Safe of the American Home Economics Association.

The competencies addressed in *Caring for Children in School-Age Programs,* as defined in the Competency Assessments, can serve as a framework as leaders in the field of school-age care work towards establishment of a national school-age staff professional development and credentialing system.

These competencies also correspond with and support the standards for quality programs outlined in *Assessing School-Age Child Care Quality (ASQ),* a self-study process developed by the School-Age Child Care Project (SACCProject) at the Center for Research on Women at Wellesley College. *ASQ* focuses on a team approach to incremental ongoing change. The *ASQ* team consists of stakeholders interested in school-age care—staff, parents, school, and community members—who share their varied perspectives. *ASQ* materials include a Leader's Manual, Questionnaires for staff, parents, and children, and a Program Observation Instrument that outlines elements of quality.

The SACCProject is designing a national system of program improvement in school-age care and exploring a partnership with NSACA to develop and administer the system. A key component of the model will be the design of national accreditation for high-quality programs. The SACCProject will work with NSACA and a national accreditation panel to establish standards for the field of school-age care based on the ASQ self-assessment instruments, then disseminate them for review by child care experts, practitioners, and child advocates.

We strongly recommend that trainers overseeing the implementation of *Caring for Children in School-Age Programs* keep informed about these two national efforts to improve school-age staff skills and program quality.

Making Training Count

Some states have specific requirements for the content, hours, and documentation of training. It is important to ensure that professional development experiences address these requirements. In addition, training experiences are more meaningful when they contribute to a school-age staff member's professional path. This means that professional development experiences should be:

- offered by a trainer who has background and experience relevant to the field of school-age care;
- conducted by an agency that is qualified to offer training (such as resource and referral agencies, vocational/technical schools, colleges, universities, child care, and NSACA); and
- documented and certified.

There are several ways to document participation in training, including college transcripts, certificates, or a training record like the one found in Appendix E. Trainers can provide copies of this record so staff can accurately document and certify their completion of professional development experiences.

II. Overseeing the Training Program

II. Overseeing the Training Program

This chapter describes:

- introducing the training program;
- completing the Orientation;
- working through a module;
- providing supportive feedback;
- what staff and trainers do to complete each module; and
- strategies for extending learning.

Introducing the Training Program

To introduce *Caring for Children in School-Age Programs*, trainers might hold a meeting to explain the purpose and importance of the program. Although all staff may not participate in the training at the same time, it is important for everyone to understand the value of the program. Once the training program is fully implemented, you can meet individually with new staff members to provide an overview of the training.

You can use the Orientation in Volume I of *Caring for Children in School-Age Programs* and the information provided in this *Trainer's Guide* to review the following topics and others specific to your situation:

- how the training meets the characteristics and circumstances of school-age staff and programs;
- the content and organization of the training modules;
- the training approach—what staff do and what the trainer does;
- how staff can benefit from completing the modules;
- the assessment process; and
- tracking progress.

It is helpful to record key points on overhead transparencies, chart paper, or a blackboard. In addition, bring copies of *Caring for Children in School-Age Programs* for staff to examine. Other suggestions for introducing the training program follow.

Invite Input on Successful Training Practices

Ask staff to describe training practices they have found to be effective, such as observation and feedback by trainers, supervisors, or colleagues; viewing videotapes; reading books or articles; watching someone else perform a task; and discussing an idea or concept. Also ask staff to indicate which areas they would most like their training to cover. Because this training program is very comprehensive, you can then show staff how their training requests have been addressed in the content and training approach used in *Caring for Children in School-Age Programs*.

Discuss the Importance of Observation

Explain that observation is a tool used by staff as they complete many of the Learning Activities in the modules. You might want to include a block of time in your agenda to review this topic and to give staff an opportunity to practice making systematic, objective observations that record facts rather than judgments or inferences. You can use Module 12, Program Management, as a resource.

Trainers also use observations throughout the training program to learn more about each staff member's involvement and interactions with children. Observation notes serve as the basis for providing feedback to staff on their progress in applying the knowledge and skills they develop as they work on each module. As each staff member begins the training program, you may find it helpful to schedule a one-hour observation of the individual working with children. If staff seem uncomfortable with being observed, begin by conducting brief observations and immediately holding a feedback conference to share what you saw and heard. As staff recognize the value of having an observer take objective notes on what takes place in the program, they are likely to become more comfortable with your presence and you can increase the length of the observation period.

Explain How You Will Conduct Feedback Conferences

The training program offers—in a sense—the best of both worlds. It is tailored to each individual's needs, but it also provides for a close working relationship between trainer and participant. Emphasize that just because staff use the materials independently does not mean they will be left alone to sink or swim. The feedback provided regularly, as described later in this chapter, is central to the success of the program.

Typically, trainers overseeing *Caring for Children in School-Age Programs* meet with staff one-on-one or with small groups who are working on the same module. These meetings are opportunities to discuss the Learning Activities and to encourage staff to support each other. Peer support can encourage staff as they work with children each day and contribute to their professional growth. Describe the purpose and frequency of feedback conferences and the approach (one-on-one or group) you plan to use.

Give Staff Copies of the Individual Tracking Form

Appendix D of this *Trainer's Guide* includes an Individual Tracking Form and a Program Tracking Form. Review the Individual Tracking Form so staff will know how to monitor their own progress. There is space for the trainer to sign off when each module is completed.

The Program Tracking Form allows trainers to keep track of the progress of an entire group. This helps in scheduling feedback sessions and assessments.

Describe How Staff Accomplishments Will Be Recognized

Emphasize that staff will receive recognition for undertaking and completing the training. Consider implementing these suggestions for providing incentives:

- Give meaningful rewards after staff complete a substantial part of the training. For example, the school-age program could offer a certificate for dinner for two donated by a local restaurant, a new game for the children, or a copy of a favorite resource.

- Hold recognition dinners and award ceremonies for staff who have completed the program, with invitations extended to spouses, parents, and other special guests.

- Organize and display scrapbooks or picture albums that can be used to introduce the school-age staff to parents interested in enrolling their children in the program. Highlight each staff member with pictures of the individual interacting and participating with children and information about his or her special interests and accomplishments.

- Offer child care so a staff member and guest can spend an evening out. Staff might volunteer their child care services to acknowledge the success of a colleague.

- Provide special pins or framed certificates acknowledging completion of part or all of the program.

- Post on a bulletin board or include in the program newsletter photographs of staff who have undertaken or completed the program.

Completing the Orientation

The program begins with an Orientation that describes the program content and format and includes two important steps: a Self-Assessment and development of an Individual Training Plan.

Self-Assessment

After staff members read the Orientation and before they begin the first module, they assess their skills by ranking how frequently they carry out basic activities identified for each module. This is not a test. It is an exercise designed to introduce the major topics and skills covered in each module and to help staff decide on which modules they will work first. Encourage staff to complete the Self-Assessment as honestly as possible. Honest answers will allow them to develop training plans that reflect their needs and interests. For some staff, trainers may want to acknowledge it can be difficult to identify the skills they need to develop further and what areas they need to know more about.

Individual Training Plan

Each staff member develops an Individual Training Plan during a one-on-one meeting with the trainer. In general, the Self-Assessment results and your observation notes serve as the basis for making decisions about the order in which a staff member will complete the modules. Try to allow enough time—15 to 30 minutes—at this meeting for a thorough discussion of the individual's skills and training goals.

It can be helpful, especially when first implementing the training program, to encourage several staff members to work on the same module at the same time. Coordinating training plans in this way allows you to conduct group feedback sessions during which staff can learn from and provide support to their colleagues. Also, group sessions make supervising the program less time-consuming for the trainer. But keep in mind that some staff may benefit from individualized feedback on modules in which their skills are less developed.

Working Through a Module

Although the content and activities in the modules vary substantially, staff follow the same process for completing each one. It can take four to six weeks to complete all the Learning Activities in a module. The entire training program takes about 12 to 18 months. Each section of a module is described below.

The Overview

The Overview introduces the three primary skills to be addressed in the module. These correspond to the basic activities listed in the Self-Assessment. Staff read background information, concrete examples of school-age staff demonstrating their competence in using each of the three primary skills, and three short vignettes, each depicting staff using a primary skill. Questions following each vignette help staff learn more about the topic. The last activity in the Overview allows staff to consider the topic in relation to their own experiences.

The Pre-Training Assessment

The Pre-Training Assessment lists the skills described in the concrete examples of staff demonstrating their competence. Staff indicate whether they do these things regularly, sometimes, or not enough, and identify three to five skills they want to improve or topics they want to know learn more about. Staff meet with the trainer to discuss their responses to the Overview and Pre-Training Assessment, then begin the Learning Activities for the module.

Learning Activities

Each module includes five to six Learning Activities. The activities begin with objectives—statements of what staff will learn—and several pages of information about the topic. After completing the reading, staff apply their knowledge in their work with children. This application may require staff to answer questions, complete a checklist, try out suggestions from the reading, involve the children in planning an activity, or observe and document children's behavior and interactions. Examples of completed forms are provided, when needed, to demonstrate how to do the activity.

After completing each Learning Activity, staff meet with the trainer to discuss the information presented and their responses. For some activities, staff review answer sheets provided at the end of the module or meet with colleagues to discuss what they did and what they learned.

Summarizing Your Progress

The last section of each module is titled, Summarizing Your Progress. After completing all the Learning Activities, staff review their responses to the Pre-Training Assessment and write a brief summary of what they have learned and the skills they have acquired. They then meet with the trainer to review progress, verify that they have successfully completed the Learning Activities, and schedule the Knowledge and Competency Assessments.

The diagram on the next page illustrates the training process.

The Training Process

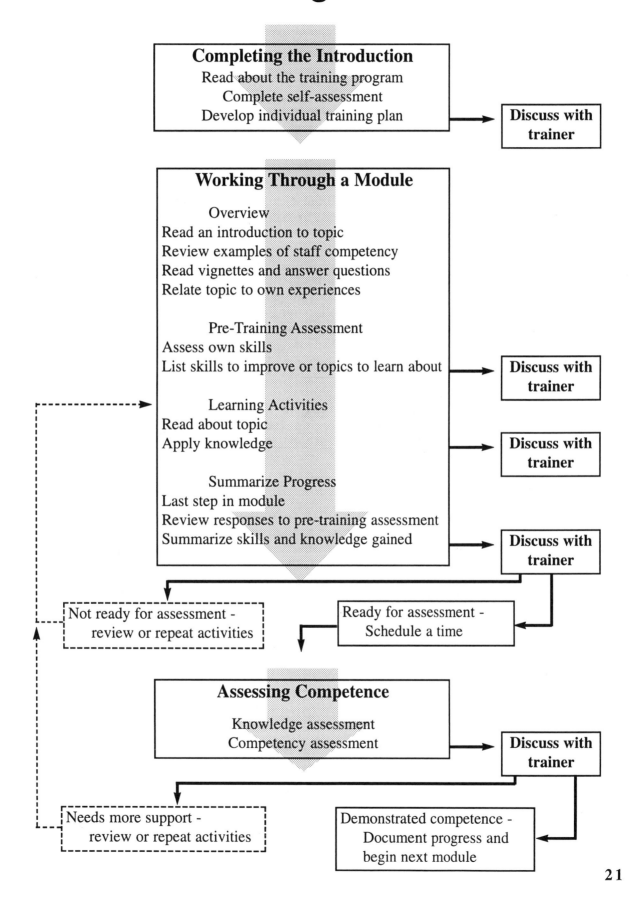

Completing the Introduction
Read about the training program
Complete self-assessment
Develop individual training plan

→ **Discuss with trainer**

Working Through a Module

Overview
Read an introduction to topic
Review examples of staff competency
Read vignettes and answer questions
Relate topic to own experiences

Pre-Training Assessment
Assess own skills
List skills to improve or topics to learn about

→ **Discuss with trainer**

Learning Activities
Read about topic
Apply knowledge

→ **Discuss with trainer**

Summarize Progress
Last step in module
Review responses to pre-training assessment
Summarize skills and knowledge gained

→ **Discuss with trainer**

Not ready for assessment - review or repeat activities

Ready for assessment - Schedule a time

Assessing Competence

Knowledge assessment
Competency assessment

→ **Discuss with trainer**

Needs more support - review or repeat activities

Demonstrated competence - Document progress and begin next module

The Assessment Process

Each module includes a Knowledge Assessment and Modules 1 through 12 have a Competency Assessment. (The assessments and guidance for their use are found in Chapter IV.)

- The Knowledge Assessment is a paper-and-pencil exercise that tests knowledge of the concepts presented in the module. Staff take this test in the trainer's presence. If a staff member does not achieve a score of at least 80 percent, note which answers were wrong and suggest that he or she review or repeat the appropriate Learning Activity and then retake the assessment.

- The Competency Assessment is a one-hour observation of the staff member working with children. The trainer uses the results of this observation—and any others conducted during the past month—to complete a module-specific list of assessment criteria. These criteria correspond to the skills listed on the Pre-Training Assessment. The trainer observes the staff member, determines whether the criteria for successful completion were met, and discusses the observation with the individual. When staff are successful, offer congratulations and encourage them to begin the next module on the Individual Training Plan. If the staff member needs to spend more time on the module, you can suggest repeating some of the Learning Activities or offer additional resources and opportunities to acquire the additional skills and knowledge.

Documentation of Progress

After staff have successfully completed the Learning Activities and both assessments, they can record their progress on the Individual Tracking Form (included in Appendix D) and ask for the trainer's sign-off. Trainers can use the Program Tracking Form (also in Appendix D) to document and monitor progress of the whole group.

Providing Feedback

Whether provided one-on-one or during group sessions, the trainer's feedback to staff is crucial to the success of *Caring for Children In School-Age Programs*. Feedback conferences are particularly important because of the self-instructional nature of the training program. These conferences give trainers regular contact with staff and allow them to answer questions, offer support during Learning Activities, make suggestions and hear concerns about progress, reinforce new skills and help staff recognize how much they have learned, and help staff repeat activities they may have misunderstood the first time.

For each module, trainers provide feedback after staff complete:

- the Overview and Pre-Training Assessment;
- each Learning Activity;
- the Summarizing Your Progress section of the module; and
- the Knowledge and Competency Assessments.

Feedback conferences may be as short as 10 minutes or may last longer, depending on how much feedback and support staff need. Try to schedule a feedback conference for *each* learning activity before the staff member goes on to the next one. To make sure the staff member has understood the content, it is always best to discuss responses while they are still fresh in his or her mind. A full understanding of each activity is particularly important when one Learning Activity builds on the results of the previous one.

Encourage staff to take the initiative in scheduling feedback conferences. You can post a schedule of times when you are free and encourage staff to sign up when ready. When several staff are working on the same module, the decision on when to meet should be a joint one, because everyone will have to be at the same point in the module at the time of the feedback conference.

Here are some suggestions for conducting one-on-one or group feedback sessions. You can adapt them to reflect your own training style and what you know about each staff member.

- **Prepare for the conference by reviewing the written responses in each Learning Activity ahead of time.** This is especially important when a trainer must give feedback on inappropriate responses. Consider carefully how to approach the session so the comments are constructive and don't discourage a staff member from trying the activity again.

- **Begin with an open-ended question.** For example, "How did you feel about this activity?" or "Were you surprised by anything you read?" Take a few minutes to discuss each staff member's responses to the questions.

- **Acknowledge accurate, appropriate responses.** For example: "I like the way you phrased that. You told him clearly what you expected, but you were careful to show him you understood his feelings."

- **Relate staff responses to information in the text.** For example: "You clearly understood the suggested strategies for handling challenging behaviors."

- **Ask questions to determine the level of difficulty.** For example:

  "Were some parts of the activity easier than others?"

  "Were there any problem areas for you?"

  "Was anything unclear or confusing?"

- **Ask questions about inappropriate responses.** Instead of simply correcting these responses, help the staff member think through why a response is inappropriate and what effect it might have on a child. For example:

  "What do you think are the reasons for Jan's behavior?"

  "How could you involve the children in planning this activity?"

  "What message would this statement give to the child?"

- **Help the staff member arrive at a more appropriate response.** You might say:

  "Let's look back at the text. Perhaps there's another way to phrase this so it offers guidance without making the child feel discouraged."

The underlying goal of providing feedback is to improve a staff member's skills and knowledge. If a staff member has not understood the information presented in the module, use the feedback conference to review and explain the information and promote understanding. Specific strategies for extending learning are included with the charts in the next section.

Incorporating Additional Resources

Professional organizations and publishers offer numerous books, journals, audiovisual productions, and training manuals related to school-age care. The Orientation in Volume I of this training program includes an extensive bibliography of resources for school-age programs. Trainers may want to suggest additional resources to staff who are having difficulty mastering the skills and knowledge in a module, or to those who want to learn more about a specific topic.

What Staff and Trainers Do in Each Module

The following charts summarize what the staff and trainers do in each section of the 13 modules. Individual staff and trainers have different learning and interaction styles. Thus, these charts do not present hard-and-fast rules to be followed inflexibly. Rather, they summarize what staff are asked to do and suggest constructive ways trainers can provide support. Each chart is followed by suggested strategies for extending learning in individual or group sessions.

Completing Module 1: Safe

Learning Activity	What Staff Members Do	What Trainers Do

Overview and Pre-Training Assessment	Read about safety and what staff can do to keep children safe.
	
	Read examples of situations in which staff ensured children's safety and answer questions.
	
	Answer questions about a personal safety experience.
	
	Complete Pre-Training Assessment and list three to five skills to improve or topics to learn more about.
	
	Discuss Overview and Pre-Training Assessment with the trainer.
		Review their ongoing written observations of staff members.
		
		Discuss with staff:
		
		    responses to questions;
		
		    personal experience feeling unsafe and how this relates to keeping children safe; and
		
		    Pre-Training Assessment.
		
		Validate where possible with their written observations.

I. Creating and Maintaining a Safe Environment	Read about safety precautions and suggestions for setting up and maintaining a safe environment. Invite children to help use check-lists to evaluate safety conditions in the indoor and outdoor environment. List unsafe items and what should be done to improve the safety of the environment. Discuss suggested improvements with children who helped complete the checklist and with the trainer.	Review the checklists and potential dangers identified. Discuss ways to make the needed changes, with children's help if appropriate.
II. Preventing Accidents Through Supervision and Planning	Read about ways to plan and supervise activities to ensure children's safety. Observe briefly and note a child's activities, identify potential hazards to child in the environment, and suggest what to do to prevent accidents. Discuss answers with a colleague.	Discuss the importance of maintaining safe adult-child ratios, monitoring children's arrivals and departures, and working with colleagues to supervise all indoor and outdoor areas. Review answers to observation activity and help staff identify additional safety precautions.

Module 1: Safe (continued)

Learning Activity	What Staff Members Do	What Trainers Do
III. Knowing and Following Emergency Procedures	Read about preparing for emergencies, first-aid procedures, and how to respond in weather-related emergencies. Read also about using a fire extinguisher. Review program's emergency and evacuation plan and answer questions about procedures for emergencies and accidents. Discuss the activity with the trainer. If questions remain, discuss with supervisor.	Review and discuss answers to emergency and accident questions. Help clarify procedures that aren't clear.
IV. Ensuring Children's Safety Away From the Program	Read about teaching children to walk safely near traffic and planning safe field trips. Record the program's rules and procedures for ensuring children's safety on field trips. Identify additional safety precautions to ensure children's safety. Discuss the activity with colleagues and the trainer.	Review the program's safety rules and procedures as recorded by staff. Encourage staff to continue teaching children to use safety precautions while away from the program. Provide additional resources and training on this topic, if needed.
V. Helping Children Keep Themselves Safe	Read about helping children to keep themselves safe by modeling, involving children in setting safety rules, discussing potential dangers, setting guidelines before new activities, and reviewing the rules for a new sport or game. Involve children in developing safety rules for an activity. Discuss the activity with the trainer.	Discuss staff member's experiences developing safety rules with children. Help staff implement additional strategies for teaching children to keep themselves safe.

Module 1: Safe (continued)

Learning Activity	What Staff Members Do	What Trainers Do
Summarizing Your Progress	Review responses to Pre-Training Assessment, summarize what was learned in this module, and list skills developed or improved.	Discuss summary of progress. Schedule assessments for this module. The Competency Assessment includes observation of an emergency drill.

Strategies for Extending Learning

- Distribute information on and encourage staff to attend safety training courses or workshops offered at the program and by national organizations such as the Red Cross or local hospitals.

- Encourage staff to write to groups such as the American Academy of Pediatrics and the Consumer Product Safety Commission (addresses are in Appendix G) for free information on keeping children safe. Suggest ways to share the information with parents.

- Brainstorm with staff ways to individualize the safety checklist to reflect the layout, furnishings, materials, and equipment in the school-age program.

- Ask the local Red Cross or fire department to provide training on how to respond during emergencies and natural disasters such as hurricanes, floods, and tornadoes.

- Put together a scrapbook highlighting actions school-age staff have taken to keep children safe in emergencies or crises.

Completing Module 2: Healthy

Learning Activity	What Staff Members Do	What Trainers Do

Overview and Pre-Training Assessment	Read about health and nutrition, signs of child abuse, and what staff can do to keep children healthy.
	
	Read examples of situations in which staff kept children healthy and responded to signs of possible abuse, and answer questions.
	
	Answer questions about personal health and nutrition habits.
	
	Complete Pre-Training Assessment and list three to five skills to improve or topics to learn more about.
	
	Discuss Overview and Pre-Training Assessment with the trainer.
		Review their ongoing written observations of staff members.
		
		Discuss with staff:
		
		    responses to questions;
		
		    personal health habits and how they relate to keeping children healthy (if staff wish to share them); and
		
		    Pre-Training Assessment.
		
		Validate where possible with their written observations.

I. Maintaining a Hygienic Environment	Read about maintaining a hygienic environment: treating lice, disinfecting materials and equipment, handwashing procedures, and recognizing symptoms of contagious diseases. Review how HIV/AIDS is transmitted. Invite children to help use a checklist to assess the program's health and hygiene routines. List items that need improvement and strategies for making changes. Make needed changes so the environment will be more hygienic and ask children to check off completed items. Discuss improvement strategies with children who helped complete the checklist and with the trainer.	Review completed checklist and items needing improvement. Meet with staff and children to discuss plan for making changes so the environment will be more hygienic. Suggest other items that might need improvement.

Module 2: Healthy (continued)

Learning Activity	What Staff Members Do	What Trainers Do
II. Encouraging Healthy Habits	Read about children's typical concerns related to body image, nutrition education, the Child and Adult Care Food Program, dental health, implementing self-service snack, serving and eating family style, and cooking with children. Plan and conduct a cooking activity, answer questions about what happened during the activity and what they might do differently next time. Discuss the activity with the trainer.	Offer to assist in collecting resources and ingredients for the cooking activity. If possible, observe staff implementing the activity. Discuss written responses to the questions and help staff plan ways to involve children in preparing meals and snacks.
III. Helping Children Cope With Stress	Read about sources of stress, healthy and unhealthy ways to handle stress, and how the program can reduce sources of stress. Observe a child over time to identify what kinds of situations are stressful for the child. Recommend ways to reduce the stress and help the child cope more effectively. Discuss the activity with colleagues and the trainer.	Discuss the types of stress children and families face and how staff can help children use healthy strategies for handling stress. Suggest that staff review the strategies for reducing stress on pages 126-128, and work with colleagues to implement any the program does not use.
IV. Recognizing Child Abuse and Neglect	Read definitions of different types of child abuse and neglect. Also, read about the signs of possible abuse or neglect and recognizing signs through conversations and interviews with parents. Read about the indicators of abuse and neglect in a school-age care setting. Answer questions about child abuse and neglect; review answer sheet at end of module. Discuss the activity with the trainer.	Ensure that staff know how child maltreatment is defined by the state and understand signs of possible child maltreatment. Review and discuss answers to child abuse questions. Clarify or extend staff understanding of specific laws or indicators of abuse.

Module 2:   Healthy (continued)

Learning Activity	What Staff Members Do	What Trainers Do
V. Reporting Suspected Cases of Child Abuse and Neglect	Read about what staff must do to report suspected cases of child abuse and neglect. Complete a chart summarizing the state and local policies on reporting child abuse and neglect. Read about overcoming barriers to reporting. Review a checklist of what to do when getting ready to file a report. Read about what to do after filing the report. Answer questions about their responsibilities for reporting child abuse and neglect. Read a case study of a child who might be a victim of abuse and describe what the staff member in the example should do. Compare answer to the one provided and discuss the activity with the trainer.	If needed, provide a copy of the program's policy and procedures for reporting child abuse and neglect. Ensure that staff understand their responsibility to report suspected child abuse or neglect and that they do not need actual proof of the abuse. Review answers to the questions and discuss how they compare to those provided at the end of the module. Answer additional questions, and help alleviate remaining concerns regarding reporting suspected cases of child abuse and neglect.
Summarizing Your Progress	Review responses to Pre-Training Assessment, summarize what was learned in this module, and list skills developed or improved.	Discuss summary of progress. Schedule assessments for this module.

Strategies for Extending Learning

- Ask staff to review and discuss their menus for snacks and meals. Recommend changes, if necessary, to ensure foods served to children meet USDA guidelines—they are high in nutrients and low in fats, salt, and sugar. For full day programs offered during the summer and school vacations, share USDA cycle menus to give guidance in planning meals.

- Suggest staff ask parents to share their favorite recipes from home. Provide materials for staff and children to turn these into picture recipe cards.

- Encourage staff to help interested children plant a vegetable garden. Once the "crops" come in, children can pick fresh vegetables for snack or meal times.

- Maintain a file of recipes and plans for simple cooking activities. Share these with staff and encourage them to maintain their own files.

- Ask staff to review their procedures for conducting routines such as handwashing, disinfecting tabletops and counters, and serving meals. Provide materials for making charts summarizing these procedures, to hang in appropriate areas of the program. The charts could be illustrated with photographs of children and staff performing these routines.

- Encourage staff to meet regularly to discuss stresses that may be affecting children and their families and to suggest strategies for offering assistance. Ask staff to share their own healthy approaches to dealing with stress.

- Review with staff, the laws and regulations for reporting child abuse and the program's procedures for reporting suspected cases.

Completing Module 3:   Program Environment

Learning Activity	What Staff Members Do	What Trainers Do
Overview and Pre-Training Assessment	Read about indoor and outdoor program environments and what staff can do to create and use them. Read examples of situations in which staff created and used environments for school-age children and answer questions. Answer questions about the effects of being in different kinds of environments. Complete Pre-Training Assessment and list three to five skills to improve or topics to learn more about. Discuss Overview and Pre-Training Assessment with the trainer.	Review their ongoing written observations of staff members and the program environment. Discuss with staff: responses to questions; personal experiences in different environments and how this relates to creating an appropriate school-age environment; and Pre-Training Assessment. Validate where possible with their written observations.
I. Understanding How Children Use the Environment	Read about the characteristics of children ages 5 to 7, 8 to 10, and 11 to 12 and how they use the environment. Observe and list examples of children in these age groups using the environment; suggest changes to better meet the needs of each age group. Discuss suggested changes with colleagues and the trainer.	Discuss the developmental characteristics of each age group and how the environment can address their needs. Discuss suggested changes and help implement ones that will improve the program.

Module 3: Program Environment (continued)

Learning Activity	What Staff Members Do	What Trainers Do
II. Creating an Indoor Environment	Read about typical interest areas in an indoor environment, how to arrange interest areas, and strategies for creating an environment in shared space. Compare and contrast two floor plans to identify the strengths and weaknesses of each. Compare answers to those on answer sheet. Review the floor plan used by the program, decide what changes are needed, and design a new floor plan. Discuss revised floor plan with colleagues and the trainer.	Discuss strengths and weaknesses of the two floor plans. Review new program floor plans. Help staff rearrange environment if changes are appropriate. Encourage regular observations of children to see how they react to changes in the environment.
III. Using the Outdoor Environment	Read about the importance of providing opportunities for children to be outdoors and how to set up an effective outdoor space. Invite children help complete a materials and equipment checklist for the outdoor environment. Discuss the completed checklist with the children who helped. Meet with colleagues and the director to pass on recommendations for improving the outdoor environment.	Review the completed checklist and discuss necessary and desired changes. Help staff think of other ways to involve children in program planning and evaluation.
IV. Selecting Materials	Review questions to consider when selecting materials for school-age children. Complete checklists of materials in the indoor interest areas and recommend additions for each area. Discuss recommended additions with colleagues and the trainer.	Discuss completed checklists and recommended additions. Discuss why adding the suggested materials will better meet the needs of the children who attend the program Offer assistance in obtaining or making recommended materials.

Module 3: Program Environment (continued)

Learning Activity	What Staff Members Do	What Trainers Do
V. Managing the Day	Read about planning a schedule that reflects children's needs and interests, including opportunities for children to do homework, and handling routines and transitions. Review criteria for an appropriate school-age program schedule. Review a sample daily schedule and note why it is appropriate. Record program's schedule, use a checklist to assess it, and suggest revisions as needed. Discuss ideas with colleagues and the trainer.	Observe the program in action. Review program's daily schedule; discuss how it is working and if changes are needed. Help revise schedule if necessary. Discuss recommended changes with staff. Discuss ways to adapt the schedule in response to children's skills and interests and to take advantage of "teachable moments." Discuss the program's approach to meeting the needs of children and parents with regard to homework.
Summarizing Your Progress	Review responses to Pre-Training Assessment, summarize what was learned in this module, and list skills developed or improved.	Discuss summary of progress. Schedule assessments for this module.

Strategies for Extending Learning

- Provide graph paper so staff can create plans depicting ideal indoor and outdoor school-age program environments. Ask staff to explain why their plans meet the needs of children better than the current environment. Coordinate with the program director to help staff implement some of the ideas in the program's environment.

- Suggest staff members work with the older children to evaluate the effectiveness of each interest area. The children could conduct a survey to find out what children of different ages like about an area, what materials they use, what they do in the area, and what would make the area more appealing. Staff and children can review their findings and implement strategies for improving the interest areas or replacing them with ones more appropriate for the children enrolled.

- Hold a workshop on adapting the environment for children with special needs. Cover the relevant requirements of the 1990 Americans With Disabilities Act (ADA) and offer specific strategies in response to the needs of children enrolled in the program. Contact the Educational Resources Information Center (ERIC) Clearinghouse on Disabilities and Gifted Children (1-800-328-0272) for information and suggested resources.

Strategies for Extending Learning (continued)

- Help staff collect "found" materials (e.g., dramatic play props, cardboard boxes, plastic containers, computer paper, fabric scraps). Model ways to involve children in deciding how to store and display the items so they are easy to get out and put away. Suggest taking pictures of the children using the items.

- Observe a staff member and children during a transition that has been problematic. Share your observation notes and help the staff member plan a different approach for handling the transition.

- Have staff brainstorm ways to involve children in creating the program environment. Discuss the suggestions, then ask staff to select several to implement immediately.

Completing Module 4: Physical

Learning Activity	What Staff Members Do	What Trainers Do
Overview and Pre-Training Assessment	Read about gross and fine motor development, the link between children's self-esteem and physical development, and what staff can do to promote children's physical development. Read examples of situations in which staff promoted physical development and answer questions. Answer questions about staying physically fit by maintaining a good posture and flexibility. Complete Pre-Training Assessment and list three to five skills to improve or topics to learn more about. Discuss Overview and Pre-Training Assessment with the trainer.	Review their ongoing written observations of staff members. Discuss with staff: responses to questions; plans to improve posture and movements; and Pre-Training Assessment. Validate where possible with their written observations.
I. Using Your Knowledge of Child Development to Encourage Physical Fitness	Read about the physical development of children ages 5 to 7, 8 to 10, and 11 to 12. For each age group, give an example of the physical development of a child and describe how to encourage children's physical fitness. Discuss the activity with the trainer.	Review examples of children in three age groups. Discuss how techniques for encouraging physical fitness vary to respond to characteristics of each age group.

Module 4: Physical (continued)

Learning Activity	What Staff Members Do	What Trainers Do
II. Observing and Planning for Children's Physical Development	Read about how children develop fine motor skills and use their senses to coordinate movements. Read examples of children using these skills, and answer questions. Read about how children develop gross motor skills. Review 21 basic gross motor skills and give an example of how each is used in program activities. Observe a child over two 3-day periods. Identify gross and fine motor skills child uses. Suggest appropriate activities for child to practice and refine skills. Discuss the activity with the trainer.	Review examples of children using fine motor skills. Discuss activities that the program could offer to teach children gross motor skills used in sports and games. Review observation notes and suggestions for appropriate activities. Encourage regular observations of all children in the program.
III. Providing a Variety of Physical Activities	Read about the importance of physical fitness and how to plan and implement a variety of activities to address the skills, needs, and interests of all children in the program. Focus on a child who is sometimes reluctant to participate in physical activities and invite the child to be a "partner" in keeping a fitness record for three days. Review both records with child and develop fitness plans to meet individual interests and needs. Try out plans for a week, then meet again to discuss results. Answer questions about what happened. Discuss activity with colleagues and the trainer.	Help staff implement additional physical activities such as the movement stations described in the activity that appeal to a wide range of children. Suggest offering a Fitness Club for interested children. They could keep fitness records and develop and carry out fitness plans.

Module 4: Physical (continued)

Learning Activity	What Staff Members Do	What Trainers Do
IV. Using the Environment to Encourage Fine Motor Skills	Read about how fine motor skills are used in everyday life and how the materials in each interest area can encourage children to use these skills. Complete chart showing how the materials in the interest areas allow children to develop and use fine motor skills. Discuss the activity with the trainer.	Discuss completed chart and suggest other materials and activities that allow children to use their fine motor skills.
V. Helping Children Develop Positive Self-Concepts Through Physical Development	Read about the relationship between physical development and positive self-concepts and how staff interactions with children can encourage a sense of success. Read about cooperative games and how they allow children to have fun without worrying about their performance. Introduce a cooperative game to a group of children, record what happens, and note how it encouraged self-esteem. Discuss the activity with the trainer.	Discuss ways to encourage children so they can feel successful, regardless of the level of their physical skills. Observe children playing cooperative games. Discuss how individual children become involved and what they appear to be learning. Suggest including cooperative games as a regular program activity.
Summarizing Your Progress	Review responses to Pre-Training Assessment, summarize what was learned in this module, and list skills developed or improved.	Discuss summary of progress. Schedule assessments for this module.

Strategies for Extending Learning

- Plan and conduct a workshop in which staff use their fine motor skills as children do. Include activities such as knitting, woodworking, doing puzzles, playing Pick-Up sticks, drawing, building with Legos, stringing beads, and playing an instrument. Discuss the small muscle skills children can develop through these and similar activities.

- Help staff plan physical fitness activities that will attract children who are usually unwilling to participate in active games and sports. Encourage staff to help children develop lifelong fitness habits.

- Ask each staff member to assume responsibility for learning and teaching his or her colleagues how to play a new game. Provide blank forms that staff can use to record:

  - a description of the game,
  - materials and equipment needed,
  - recommended ages,
  - rules and guidelines, and
  - ways to vary the game to involve a wide range of ages and abilities.

  Include the completed forms in a notebook so staff will have an easy reference guide.

- Observe children about whom staff are concerned—children who seem to have unusual delays in fine or gross motor skill development. Discuss your observations with staff, and, if needed, with the children's parents. Encourage parents to arrange for professional follow-up, if necessary.

Completing Module 5:   Cognitive

Learning Activity	What Staff Members Do	What Trainers Do

Overview and Pre-Training Assessment	Read about theories of cognitive development and what staff can do to guide children's cognitive development.
	
	Read examples of situations in which staff guided children's cognitive development and answer questions.
	
	Read about learning styles and factors that affect the ability to learn. List factors that have helped them be successful learners.
	
	Complete Pre-Training Assessment and list three to five skills to improve or topics to learn more about.
	
	Discuss Overview and Pre-Training Assessment with the trainer.
		Review their ongoing written observations of staff members.
		
		Discuss with staff:
		
		    responses to questions;
		
		    individual learning styles and how this relates to helping children become lifelong learners; and
		
		    Pre-Training Assessment.
		
		Validate where possible with their written observations.

I. Using Your Knowledge of Child Development to Guide Cognitive Development	Read about the development of thinking and reasoning skills during the school-age years. Complete charts showing what children are like at different ages and how staff can use this information to guide cognitive development. Discuss charts with the trainer. Continue adding to them while working on the module.	Provide examples of the many ways children use cognitive skills in activities and interest areas, and while playing and working with others. Review examples of staff guiding cognitive development. Share their observations of times when staff provided opportunities for children to use cognitive skills. Encourage staff to add to the chart while working on the module.

Module 5:   Cognitive (continued)

Learning Activity	What Staff Members Do	What Trainers Do
II. Helping Children Understand the World	Read about how children pass through four stages of a learning cycle as they gain new knowledge and skills. Review suggestions for supporting children at each stage. Complete observations of three children of different ages as they work on an activity or interact with others. Note the stage at which children might be in their thinking and ways to support their cognitive growth. Discuss observations with colleagues and the trainer.	Discuss observation notes and answers to questions. Encourage staff to conduct frequent, brief observations of children to better understand what they are thinking and how they are learning about the world. If possible, observe and watch what children are doing and saying. Share examples with staff that show how children are expanding their thinking.
III. Asking Questions To Promote Children's Thinking Skills	Read about the thinking skills children develop and use throughout their lives and how to ask open-ended questions to encourage and extend children's thinking. Keep notes for a week on times children demonstrate thinking skills. Record these on a chart along with questions staff member asked to promote thinking and learning. Discuss the activity with the trainer.	Offer examples from their own observations of children using thinking skills. Review and discuss completed chart. If necessary, help rephrase questions to make them open-ended. Observe staff and give praise and suggestions for ways to further expand thinking and learning skills. Model use of questioning by asking open-ended questions related to the activity.

Module 5: Cognitive (continued)

Learning Activity	What Staff Members Do	What Trainers Do
IV. Using the Physical Environment to Promote Cognitive Development	Read about creating an environment and providing materials that encourage children to observe and explore concepts, relationships, and ideas. For each interest area and outdoors, list at least three materials to promote cognitive growth. Discuss materials with colleagues and the trainer. Offer additional suggestions to supervisor. Make changes as appropriate.	Discuss their own observations of how the environment supports children's thinking skills. Review the suggested materials and provide additional suggestions if they are not mentioned. Help make appropriate changes.
V. Helping Children Learn to Solve Problems	Read about the importance of problem-solving skills, what staff can do to help children develop and use them, and how to use the steps in the scientific method for problem solving. Select three children from different age groups. Help each child learn to use the scientific method of problem solving. Record the problem, possible solutions, evaluation and testing, and reflections on the process. Discuss the activity with the trainer.	Discuss when it is a good idea to intervene and when it is best to allow children to solve their own problems. Suggest using the steps in the scientific method to solve problems that arise at the program. Review completed examples. Discuss how the approaches used by staff were tailored to the age and characteristics of each child.
Summarizing Your Progress	Review charts from Learning Activity I and add examples to them. Review responses to Pre-Training Assessment, summarize what was learned in this module, and list skills developed or improved.	Discuss summary of progress. Schedule assessments for this module.

Strategies for Extending Learning

- Offer a workshop for both staff and parents on Howard Gardner's theories of multiple intelligences. Encourage staff and parents to offer examples of how individual children have demonstrated strong potential in specific areas. Ask staff to review their materials and activities to make sure the program provides opportunities for children to explore their interests and talents in each area of intelligence.

- During visits to the program, model ways of questioning children to extend their thinking. For example, "Can you tell me what happened on your field trip?" "Why do you think the sand doesn't fall out of the mini-vacuum?"

- Suggest staff establish a schedule for regularly assessing how well the materials in interest areas promote children's cognitive skills. If they find things that are either too challenging or not challenging enough, they can replace them with more appropriate materials.

- Involve staff in a hands-on, active learning experience to demonstrate how adults—as well as children—pass through the four stages in the learning cycle when they gain new knowledge and skills. The learning experience could be related to the job or to a life skill, such as learning to program a VCR or use a computer program.

Completing Module 6: Communication

Learning Activity	What Staff Members Do	What Trainers Do

Overview and Pre-Training Assessment	Read about communication and language skills and what staff can do to promote children's communication skills.
	
	Read examples of situations in which staff promoted children's communication skills and answer questions.
	
	Complete a checklist on personal communication skills.
	
	Complete Pre-Training Assessment and list three to five skills to improve or topics to learn more about.
	
	Discuss Overview and Pre-Training Assessment with the trainer.
		Review their ongoing written observations of staff members.
		
		Discuss with staff:
		
		    responses to questions;
		
		    self-assessment of communication skills and how this relates to promoting children's communication skills; and
		
		    Pre-Training Assessment.
		
		Validate where possible with their written observations.

I. Using Your Knowledge of Child Development to Promote Communication Skills	Read about the development of communication skills during the school-age years. Complete charts showing what children are like at different ages and how staff can use this information to promote communication skills. Discuss charts with the trainer. Continue adding to them while working on the module.	Discuss ways children use communication skills at the program. Review examples of staff promoting communication skills. Share their observations of times when staff provided opportunities for children to use their communication skills. Encourage staff to add to the chart while working on the module.

Module 6: Communication (continued)

Learning Activity	What Staff Members Do	What Trainers Do
II. Helping Children Develop Communication Skills	Read about four areas of language development and how school-age programs can provide opportunities for children to use listening, speaking, reading, and writing skills. Complete four observations—one for each area of language development—and observation summary forms. Discuss the observation results with colleagues and the trainer.	Observe one or more of the children a staff member is observing. Focus on the same area of language development as the staff member, or on another area. Compare and contrast your observation notes with the staff member. Review and discuss observation summaries.
III. Using The Physical Environment to Promote Communication Skills	Read about how to set up the environment to help children develop communication skills. For each interest area and outdoors, list at least three suggested materials or design considerations to promote communication skills. Discuss suggestions with colleagues and the trainer. Make changes as appropriate.	Discuss their own observations of how the environment supports children's development and use of communication skills. Review the suggested materials and design considerations. Help make appropriate changes.
IV. Encouraging a Love of Reading	Read about selecting books and magazines that reflect the skills and interests of school-age children. Review suggestions for encouraging children to read. Plan and implement a shared reading experience for a child in the program. Answer questions related to selecting and using a book with the child. Discuss the activity with the trainer and the child's parents.	Suggest books and magazines that would be appropriate for the children and ways to use these materials effectively. Discuss experiences selecting a book and reading with the child and conversations with the child's parents. Suggest repeating this activity with other children to get to know them and to encourage them to read for pleasure.

Module 6: Communication (continued)

Learning Activity	What Staff Members Do	What Trainers Do
V. Helping Children Communicate Their Ideas and Feelings	Read about ways to encourage children to talk and write about their ideas and feelings. Help children become sensitive to the messages sent by body language and other nonverbal behavior. Focus on a child who seems to have difficulty communicating ideas and feelings. Describe the child's skills and develop strategies for helping the child communicate more effectively. Discuss the activity with colleagues and the trainer.	Discuss why being able to communicate thoughts and feelings is an important lifelong communication skill. Observe the child who is the focus of the activity. Share their observation notes. Discuss the child's communication skills and proposed strategies. Support staff in implementing the strategies that seem most appropriate.
Summarizing Your Progress	Review charts from Learning Activity I and add examples to them. Review responses to Pre-Training Assessment, summarize what was learned in this module, and list skills developed or improved.	Discuss summary of progress. Schedule assessments for this module.

Strategies for Extending Learning

- Ask staff if you can make an audio or videotape of their conversations with children. Listen to or watch the tape together, and discuss ways to promote children's communication skills.

- Offer a workshop on signs that indicate a child might be experiencing a speech or language delay. Establish procedures for coordinating with the child's family and school. For example, the school-age program might provide enrichment activities or otherwise support the child's needs.

- Suggest staff members keep track for one day of all the times they use and model speaking, listening, reading, and writing skills, beginning in the morning when they greet children. Have them review their daily logs and think of ways to include more children in these activities. For example, they could ask older children to read to younger ones or invite children to make labels for different sections of the bulletin board.

- During visits to the school-age program, model your own love of reading by holding shared reading experiences with children.

Completing Module 7: Creative

Learning Activity	What Staff Members Do	What Trainers Do

Overview and Pre-Training Assessment	Read about creativity and what staff can do to promote children's creativity.
	
	Read examples of situations in which staff promoted children's creativity and answer questions.
	
	Complete several exercises to stimulate creative thinking.
	
	Complete Pre-Training Assessment and list three to five skills to improve or topics to learn more about.
	
	Discuss Overview and Pre-Training Assessment with the trainer.
		Review their ongoing written observations of staff members.
		
		Discuss with staff:
		
		    responses to questions;
		
		    responses to creative thinking exercises and how this relates to encouraging children's creativity; and
		
		    Pre-Training Assessment.
		
		Validate where possible with their written observations.

I. Using Your Knowledge of Child Development to Encourage Creativity	Read about how children ages 5 to 7, 8 to 10, and 11 to 12, use their creativity to explore concepts and to express their ideas and feelings. Keep a log for three days of ways they encouraged children's creativity. Discuss the activity with the trainer.	Review examples of what staff did and how their actions encouraged creativity. Share their observations of times when staff members encouraged creativity. Encourage staff to reflect on their actions and plan ways to continue encouraging children's creativity.

Module 7: Creative (continued)

Learning Activity	What Staff Members Do	What Trainers Do
II. Motivating Children to Be Creative	Read about the elements of creativity and characteristics of school-age programs that motivate children and support creativity. Use a checklist to assess how well the program environment and human interactions support children's creativity. Provide an explanation for each rating. Meet with colleagues to share and discuss assessment results and possible changes to the program. Discuss the activity with the trainer.	Discuss the reading and answer any questions. If asked, assist staff in completing the assessment. If possible, participate in the meeting to discuss the assessment results and to plan needed changes. Continue providing suggestions on how to create a program atmosphere that values and supports creative expression.
III. Supporting Children's Long-Term Projects	Read an example demonstrating how children pass through the four steps in the creative process as they participate in a long-term project. Keep a journal describing a long-term project and noting how they supported children. The journal can be completed as they proceed with other Learning Activities. Review journal entries and discuss with the trainer.	Discuss how staff provide different levels and types of support for long-term projects, depending on children's requests and whether they need coaxing to get to the next step. If possible, observe children working on their project. Read and discuss journal entries. Stress the importance of giving children sufficient space and time to carry out their plans. Encourage staff to continue supporting long-term projects.

Module 7: Creative (continued)

Learning Activity	What Staff Members Do	What Trainers Do
IV. Planning and Conducting Activities That Encourage Creativity	Read about planning, setting up, and conducting activities that provide opportunities for children to use creativity. Review suggestions for activities. Plan and conduct an activity. Answer questions about planning, setting up, and conducting the activity and describe what happened after the activity. Discuss the activity with the trainer.	Help staff understand the importance of remaining flexible and allowing children to make and carry out their own plans during an activity. If possible, observe the activity and provide feedback. Discuss what it means to facilitate children's involvement as opposed to telling them what to do. Read and discuss answers to questions about the activity.
V. Filling the Environment With Open-Ended Materials That Promote Creativity	Read about open-ended materials, examples of children using them in creative work, and why coloring books, dittos, and craft kits do not encourage creativity. List three open-ended materials found in each interest area and outdoors. Explain how the materials encourage creativity. Discuss the activity with colleagues and the trainer.	Help staff collect "beautiful junk" that can be used by children in many different ways. Review the examples of open-ended materials and offer additional suggestions of items the program could provide. Meet with staff to discuss what the program can do to make sure there are stimulating materials in all interest areas and outdoors.
Summarizing Your Progress	Review responses to Pre-Training Assessment, summarize what was learned in this module, and list skills developed or improved.	Discuss summary of progress. Schedule assessments for this module.

Strategies for Extending Learning

• Offer a hands-on, open-ended workshop on the creative process. Provide a wide variety of materials and resources and encourage staff to get fully involved in the creative process. Help them resist focusing on what might be products of their creative work. At the end of the workshop, ask participants to discuss how they moved back and forth between and among the stages, focusing again on the process—rather than the results—of using their creativity.

• Encourage staff to identify what they really love to do—the areas where their domain skills, creative thinking and working skills, and intrinsic motivation overlap. Help them plan ways to explore their own creativity in these areas.

• Suggest staff help children take photographs to create a visual record of the different stages of a long-term project. Photos can be displayed in an album or on a bulletin board. Staff can ask open-ended questions to help children recall what they did at different stages, think about the effects of their actions, and consider what might have happened if they did things differently. Ideally, the photos will provide a visual record of risk-taking and what is learned from trying different options.

• Help staff develop a checklist to assess how well the activities they plan and implement support creativity. Individuals can use the checklist to evaluate an activity—involving children as appropriate.

• Ask staff to think of a time during their childhood when an adult supported their creativity. List on chart paper what the adults did to encourage creativity. Next, ask staff to think of a time when an adult prevented them from being creative. List on chart paper the adult actions that got in the way of their creativity. Use the two lists to discuss how staff can actively encourage children's creative efforts.

Completing Module 8: Self

Learning Activity	What Staff Members Do	What Trainers Do
Overview and Pre-Training Assessment	Read about how a sense of self develops and how staff can foster children's sense of self and self-esteem. Read examples of situations in which staff fostered children's sense of competence and esteem and answer questions. Answer questions about the experiences that contributed to their own sense of self and values. Complete Pre-Training Assessment and list three to five skills to improve or topics to learn more about. Discuss Overview and Pre-Training Assessment with the trainer.	Review their ongoing written observations of staff members. Discuss with staff: responses to questions; experiences that contributed to their values, expectations, and sense of self and how they relate to helping children feel good about themselves; and Pre-Training Assessment. Validate where possible with their written observations.
I. Using Your Knowledge of Child Development to Foster Self-Esteem	Read about Erikson's stages of socio-emotional development and how staff can foster children's self-esteem. Give examples of typical behavior of children at different ages and how staff can respond to foster their self-esteem. Discuss the activity with the trainer.	Discuss the stages of socio-emotional development and how they are related to self-esteem. Review examples of typical behaviors and staff responses. Provide additional examples from their own observations and experiences. Encourage continued reflection on ways to help every child develop self-esteem.

Module 8: Self (continued)

Learning Activity	What Staff Members Do	What Trainers Do
II. Observing Individual Children	Read about using observation to get to know children as individuals. Select a child to observe for 5 to 10 minutes. Conduct observation, then use notes to answer questions about the child's behavior. Plan to observe and get to know the other children in program. Discuss the activity with colleagues and the trainer.	Discuss answers to questions about the child. Share their own observations if appropriate. Encourage staff to use observation to get to know all the children and to use information gained through observations to foster children's self-esteem.
III. Responding to Each Child as an Individual	Read about getting to know and understand each child as a unique individual, recognizing factors that affect a child's temperament, and responding to children with diagnosed learning disabilities. Select a child with whom they find it difficult to work or whose behavior is hard to understand. Answer questions about the child's behavior and about personal characteristics that may affect their interactions with the child. Plan and implement three strategies for getting to know the child. Summarize what was learned about the child and how they can use the information to foster a sense of self and self-esteem. Discuss the activity with colleagues and the trainer.	Provide information or assistance, if appropriate, related to working with children with a specific diagnosed learning disability. Discuss responses to questions and staff members' difficulties understanding and relating to the child. Discuss strategies used and if they were or were not successful. Help staff implement other strategies if necessary. Help staff understand the importance of accepting and valuing every child, regardless of personal feelings.

Module 8: Self (continued)

Learning Activity	What Staff Members Do	What Trainers Do
IV. Talking to Children in Ways That Show Respect	Read about the importance of listening carefully and using positive and supportive words that communicate respect when talking with children. Write what a staff member might say to respond to children in different typical situations. Tape-record or videotape, if possible, themselves talking with children. Discuss the activity with the trainer. If conversations were recorded or videotaped, review with the trainer and discuss children's verbal and nonverbal reactions.	Acknowledge use of positive and supportive words. Provide encouragement and feedback as staff members begin to change their style of communication. Offer feedback and model speaking to children in respectful ways. Help interested staff gain access to a tape recorder or video camera. Discuss written responses to children in typical situations. If necessary, help staff rewrite them in positive terms. Encourage staff member to make and display several signs listing positive words to use as reminders for children and staff.
V. Promoting Children's Sense of Competence	Read about how children develop a sense of competence. Also, read about providing the right level of support as children learn new things, creating an environment that builds a sense of competence, and planning for a wide range of abilities and interests. Focus on one child and assess whether four conditions that contribute to self-esteem are present. Then plan ways the program can provide the conditions to help all children experience a sense of competence. Discuss the activity with colleagues and the trainer.	Discuss ways to help children feel competent and successful. Review and give feedback on what the program can do to provide experiences that contribute to children's sense of competence. Suggest repeating the activity to assess all children in the program. Encourage continued use of observations and suggest ways to offer appropriate levels of support to children.
Summarizing Your Progress	Review responses to Pre-Training Assessment, summarize what was learned in this module, and list skills developed or improved.	Discuss summary of progress. Schedule assessments for this module.

Strategies for Extending Learning

- Ask staff for their suggestions of new materials that would offer greater challenges, allow children to use skills not being used, or provide greater variety.

- Work with interested staff and the director to plan and offer a joint workshop for parents and staff on the relationship between high self-esteem and children's ability to resist inappropriate behaviors, such as early sexual activity and substance abuse.

- Suggest the staff have children make books depicting what they do at the school-age program. Books can be illustrated by children, include photographs, or feature a combination of the two. Older children might prefer to work as a group to show what they do at the program. These books could be shared with new parents and older children who are reluctant to come to the program because they think there won't be enough activities for their age group.

- Have staff list the planning, preparation, clean-up, administrative, and other tasks involved in operating the program. Ask them to think of ways they could involve the children in completing these tasks—to help children feel competent and to free up staff time for more meaningful roles with children.

- Have staff think back to the people (parents, teachers, counselors, relatives) who made them feel especially good about themselves. Ask them to picture themselves interacting with one of these people. Use the following questions to lead a discussion about how adults can help children feel competent:

  - What did this person do or say to help you feel good about yourself?
  - How did you feel about yourself at the time?
  - How has this experience affected your sense of competence?

Completing Module 9:   Social

Learning Activity	What Staff Members Do	What Trainers Do

Overview and Pre-Training Assessment	Read about social development and what staff can do to promote children's social skills.
	
	Read examples of situations in which staff promoted social development and answer questions.
	
	Give examples to show how they use and model social skills.
	
	Complete Pre-Training Assessment and list three to five skills to improve or topics to learn more about.
	
	Discuss Overview and Pre-Training Assessment with the trainer.
		Review their ongoing written observations of staff members.
		
		Discuss with staff:
		
		    responses to questions;
		
		    experiences modeling social skills and how children can learn from staff; and
		
		    Pre-Training Assessment.
		
		Validate where possible with their written observations.

I. Using Your Knowledge of Child Development to Promote Social Development	Read about the socio-emotional development of school-age children as described by Dr. Stanley Greenspan. Provide examples of the behaviors of children in the program related to the developmental characteristics of three age groups. Discuss charts with the trainer.	Discuss the three stages of development described by Greenspan and offer examples from their observations of children. Review completed charts and discuss what staff can do to support children.
II. Promoting Children's Play	Read about the types of play typical of school-age children and what staff can do to encourage children's social development through play. Use a checklist to assess how the program supports children's play. Review the results and plan ways to improve the program environment and encourage children's play. Share experiences with the trainer and develop plans for improving the environment.	Discuss the kinds of play staff have seen children of different ages engaged in. Discuss various ways to build on children's interests for an extended period of time. Encourage staff to continue to assess the environment and their own practices that promote children's play.

Module 9: Social (continued)

Learning Activity	What Staff Members Do	What Trainers Do
III. Promoting Children's Emotional Development	Read about emotional milestones school-age children master, as defined by Dr. Stanley Greenspan. Review techniques staff can use to support emotional development. Give examples of how they use these techniques. Observe and keep a journal for five days noting use of techniques for promoting emotional development and how the children responded. Discuss journal entries with colleagues and the trainer.	Share examples of times they have seen staff encourage children. Read and discuss journal entries with staff. Emphasize how techniques vary, depending on children's ages and unique characteristics.
IV. Helping Children Relate Positively to Others	Read about helping all children (especially shy, overly aggressive, or rejected children) make friends. Observe a child who needs help learning to make friends. Develop and implement a plan for helping the child develop friendships. Describe the results after one week. Discuss with the trainer how interventions helped the child develop friendships.	Discuss children who may be having trouble making friends. Review observation notes, plan, and results. Offer feedback and suggestions. Discuss the importance of helping children learn to make friends. Encourage continued interventions with children who need assistance.
V. Building a Sense of Community	Read about promoting a sense of community in the program and encouraging children to be involved in the larger community. Plan and implement a strategy to involve children in the community at large. Describe what happened. Discuss the activity with colleagues and the trainer.	Review strategy for involving children in the community and help with the implementation if necessary. Discuss activity and encourage use of other strategies for community involvement with the children throughout the year.

Module 9:   Social (continued)

Summarizing Your Progress	Review charts from Learning Activity I and add examples to them. Review responses to Pre-Training Assessment, summarize what was learned in this module, and list skills developed or improved.	Discuss summary of progress. Schedule assessments for this module.

Strategies for Extending Learning

- Offer a workshop on play. Highlight the book, *Facilitating Play,* by Sara Smilansky and Leah Shefatya and their theory on the relationship between sociodramatic play and later academic achievement.

- Assist staff who want to work with parents to locate professional help for a child who seems to be experiencing severe problems getting along with others.

- Have staff do a sociogram on the children in the program—focusing on one or all age groups. What roles emerge? Do any of the observations indicate a child's behavior needs attention? For example, does one child often have difficulty getting included in activities?

- Encourage staff to continue using Greenspan's techniques to help children master socio-emotional milestones. If appropriate, model the techniques when you visit the program and lead role-plays so staff can experience using them in a safe setting. Conduct observations of staff using the techniques, then offer an objective report of what you saw and heard and how it helped the child.

- Discuss and plan ways to get children involved in community projects and events, and in learning about how their community functions.

- Suggest staff work with the children to create prop boxes such as the ones described at the end of the module.

Completing Module 10:   Guidance

Learning Activity	What Staff Members Do	What Trainers Do
Overview and Pre-Training Assessment	Read about helping children develop self-discipline and what staff can do to guide children's behavior. Read examples of situations in which staff guided children's behavior and answer questions. Answer questions about personal self-discipline experiences. Complete Pre-Training Assessment and list three to five skills to improve or topics to learn more about. Discuss Overview and Pre-Training Assessment with the trainer.	Review their ongoing written observations of staff members. Discuss with staff: responses to questions; personal experiences related to self-discipline and how they relate to helping children gain self-discipline; and Pre-Training Assessment. Validate where possible with their written observations.
I. Using Your Knowledge of Child Development to Guide Behavior	Read about the stages of moral development and the reasons for children's behavior at each stage. Complete charts showing what children are like at different ages and how staff can promote self-discipline. Discuss charts with the trainer. Continue adding to them while working on the module.	Discuss the stages of moral development and how this information can be used in interactions with children. Review examples of staff promoting self-discipline. Share their observations of times when staff used positive guidance to help children learn self-discipline. Encourage staff to add to the charts while working on the module.

Module 10: Guidance (continued)

Learning Activity	What Staff Members Do	What Trainers Do
II. Creating an Environment that Supports Self-Discipline	Read about the physical and social elements of the environment that support children's activities and prevent behavior problems. Complete a chart about five common behavior problems, possible problems in the environment, and ways to change the environment to alleviate the problem behaviors. Compare answers to those on answer sheet at the end of the module. Discuss the activity with the trainer.	Compare the examples of how the physical and social environment can support children's positive behavior to the program's environment. Suggest changes if necessary. Review completed chart and analysis of the environment and compare to answer sheet. Discuss how the proposed changes could improve children's behavior.
III. Guiding Children's Behavior	Read about the differences between discipline and punishment and how self-discipline is used in many areas of life. Read how children express their feelings through behavior. Finally, read about suggested positive guidance approaches. Keep track of how they guide the behavior of an individual child over a five-day period. Record what the child does and their responses. Plan ways to use this information to help the child develop self-discipline. Discuss the activity with the trainer.	Discuss the differences between discipline and punishment. Make sure staff understand why it is important to help children develop self-discipline—a skill used throughout life. Review observations and highlight instances when staff used positive guidance techniques. Encourage continued observation of children to determine their needs and to select guidance techniques appropriate for each child and situation.

Module 10: Guidance (continued)

Learning Activity	What Staff Members Do	What Trainers Do
IV. Teaching Children to Use Conflict Resolution Techniques	Read about the causes of conflicts, how a well-designed school-age program can reduce them, and suggested conflict resolution techniques. Answer questions about a conflict observed in the program, the conflict resolution techniques they used or taught to children, and the results. Discuss the activity with colleagues and the trainer.	Discuss the description of a school-age program in which conflicts are reduced. Does it describe your program? What changes might be needed to reduce the potential for conflicts? Review answers to questions. Discuss the effect of the technique, whether children could now use it on their own, and which techniques are most appropriate for the children in the program. Encourage continued use of conflict resolution techniques, including new ones developed by staff and children.
V. Involving Children in Setting Rules and Limits	Read about the effects of stating rules in positive rather than negative terms, involving children in creating rules, and the importance of reviewing and revising rules as children mature and gain new skills. List the program's rules. Select one rule and answer questions about why it exists and how it is applied. Discuss the activity with the trainer.	Discuss personal reactions to rules—at work, at home, and in society at large. Discuss the lessons children learn from being involved in making rules—this is the basis of a participatory democracy. Help establish a schedule for regular review of rules to respond to children's changing needs.

Module 10:   Guidance (continued)

Learning Activity	What Staff Members Do	What Trainers Do
VI. Responding to Challenging Behaviors	Read about children's challenging behaviors and some probable reasons for them. Think of a child who has a challenging behavior. Describe the child's behavior and how they usually respond. Ask the child's parents to participate in the activity. Work with them to develop a joint plan for responding to the behavior. Implement the plan and evaluate the results. Discuss the activity with the trainer.	Discuss the meaning of "challenging behavior" and why this term is used instead of "problem behavior." If possible, observe the child with the challenging behavior and share their notes and perceptions. If asked, help staff prepare for discussion with the child's parents. Help implement the strategy for dealing with the challenging behavior. Check back regularly to discuss whether it is effective. Reinforce continued use of positive guidance to respond to challenging behaviors.
Summarizing Your Progress	Review charts from Learning Activity I and add examples to them. Review responses to Pre-Training Assessment, summarize what was learned in this module, and list skills developed or improved.	Discuss summary of progress. Schedule assessments for this module.

Strategies for Extending Learning

- Use the information in this module and others to make a large chart showing the developmental stages through which school-age children pass. Post the chart where all staff can see it, for example in the room used for breaks. Next to the chart, post a sheet of paper with the question, "How can you use this information to encourage self-discipline?" Ask staff to write their suggestions and comment on each other's. Discuss the suggestions at a staff meeting and implement those that seem most useful.

- Sponsor a workshop for parents and staff to discuss typical behaviors of children and appropriate positive guidance techniques that can be used at home. Help staff plan an agenda and decide the key ideas to be shared with parents.

- Ask staff if you can tape-record or videotape their conversations and interactions with children. Listen to or view the tape together to identify words used to guide children's behavior. Staff can use the equipment for an additional week to hear how they have increased their use of positive words.

- Have staff role-play how to respond to challenging behaviors such as hitting, lying, talking back, or cursing. (The role-plays should address the staff's immediate response to the child, as opposed to the long-term strategies they would use to work with the parents to find the cause of the behavior and to develop strategies for addressing it.)

Completing Module 11: Families

Learning Activity	What Staff Members Do	What Trainers Do
Overview and Pre-Training Assessment	Read about how staff and parents work as a team and what staff do in their work with families. Read examples of situations in which staff worked with families and answer questions. Answer questions about the differences between the families they grew up in and today's typical families. Complete Pre-Training Assessment and list three to five skills to improve or topics to learn more about. Discuss Overview and Pre-Training Assessment with the trainer.	Review their ongoing written observations of staff members. Discuss with staff: responses to questions; experiences in their families and how theirs affect partnerships with parents; and Pre-Training Assessment. Validate where possible with their written observations.
I. Developing a Partnership with Parents	Read about establishing and maintaining strong partnerships with parents. Tape-record or take notes on interactions with parents of a child in the program for two weeks. Record information shared and ways that the partnership helped the child. Discuss the activity with child's parents and with the trainer.	Observe interactions between staff and parents. Give objective accounts of what was said and the nonverbal communication that took place. Review and discuss notes on interactions with family. Give feedback and make suggestions for improving relationships, if necessary. Suggest completing an abbreviated version of the activity with the parents of other children in the program. Discuss activity with individual staff and the child's parents.

Module 11: Families (continued)

Learning Activity	What Staff Members Do	What Trainers Do
II. Keeping Parents Informed About the Program	Read about the importance of using a variety of communication techniques to keep parents informed about the program. Answer questions about a technique the program uses to keep parents informed. Suggest, try out, and report on ideas for improving this technique. Discuss the activity with the trainer.	Read newsletters, notices, and so forth that the program uses to keeps parents informed. Discuss tone, language level, and cultural sensitivity. Review responses to questions concerning communication technique. Discuss new ways to communicate with parents.
III. Providing Ways for Parents to Be Involved	Read about a variety of parent involvement options. Plan and implement a parent involvement strategy. Review the results of the strategy and develop plans to follow up. Discuss the activity with colleagues and the trainer.	Encourage staff to ask parents how they would like to be involved in the program. Review parent involvement strategies, providing reinforcement and suggestions. Offer to help get supplies if needed. Help set realistic expectations for parent involvement.
IV. Planning and Participating in Parent-Staff Conferences	Read about the goals of parent-staff conferences and how to plan and participate in them. Plan a parent-staff conference by completing planning form, summarizing the child's development, and listing suggested goals for the next six months. Hold the conference and set goals for the next six months. Complete a conference evaluation form summarizing what happened and the information shared. Discuss the activity with the trainer.	Discuss the importance of holding regular conferences to discuss a child in depth. Help staff prepare by reviewing the planning forms and role-playing what might take place. If possible, attend the conference. Then, give feedback on the tone, body language, information shared, and overall success of the interactions. Discuss staff member's feelings about the conference. Remind staff that they will relate differently to each parent, and help them practice several communication techniques.

Module 11: Families (continued)

Learning Activity	What Staff Members Do	What Trainers Do
V. Reaching Out to Families	Read about recognizing when parents are under stress, helping parents locate resources, and giving parents information and guidance on the developmental stages of school-age children. Report on times they reached out to parents in response to requests or because it seemed parents needed support. Describe the problem, what was asked for or was needed, their response, and the outcome. Discuss the activity with the trainer.	Review examples, offer feedback, and answer questions about supporting families under stress. Reinforce policies on referrals and confidentiality. Discuss signs of stress in children, and encourage making regular observations. Discuss instances when it is appropriate to discuss a situation with the supervisor and/or refer a family for professional assistance.
Summarizing Your Progress	Review responses to Pre-Training Assessment, summarize what was learned in this module, and list skills developed or improved.	Discuss summary of progress. Schedule assessments for this module. The Competency Assessment should take place at drop-off or pick-up time when parents are at the program.

Strategies for Extending Learning

- Lead a discussion on similarities and differences between the families staff grew up in and today's families (from the module Overview). Research and provide statistics reflecting today's families—for example, how many parents are single parents, how many families include two working spouses, how many families include children from previous marriages, how many families live far away from their own parents and siblings.

- Provide information on signs and symptoms of typical problems faced by families (substance use, spouse abuse, depression) so staff are aware of them. Ask representatives from appropriate agencies to make a presentation on how to respond when it appears that a parent has a problem needing immediate attention. Develop a list of community and state organizations that provide services to families (e.g., hotlines and support groups).

Strategies for Extending Learning (continued)

- Hold a workshop on the cultures represented in the program's families and how to provide a program that values and responds to diversity.

- Conduct an informal survey of all parents to find out what kinds of information they would like to receive from the school-age program and in what form (newsletters, informal chats, phone calls, bulletin board). The survey can also ask parents what information about their children they would like to share with staff.

Completing Module 12: Program Management

Learning Activity	What Staff Members Do	What Trainers Do

Overview and Pre-Training Assessment	Read about the management tasks completed by school-age staff.
	
	Read examples of situations in which staff effectively managed the program and answer questions.
	
	Complete a chart on frustrating situations in daily life and their plans to improve them.
	
	Complete Pre-Training Assessment and list three to five skills to improve or topics to learn more about.
	
	Discuss Overview and Pre-Training Assessment with the trainer.
		Review their ongoing written observations of staff members.
		
		Discuss with staff:
		
		    responses to questions;
		
		    completed charts and plans for improvement; and
		
		    Pre-Training Assessment.
		
		Validate where possible with their written observations.

I. Using a Systematic Approach to Observing and Recording	Read about why it is important to conduct observations and guidelines for systematic and objective observations. Review examples of observations that are objective and accurate and those that are not. Read about checking the accuracy of observations. Select a child to observe daily for a one-week period. Ask the director, a colleague, or trainer to observe the child at least twice at the same time. Compare recordings after each joint observation and at the end of the week. Discuss the activity with the trainer. Repeat activity if needed.	If possible, conduct (and then discuss) at least two observations of the child at the same time as the staff member. If this is not possible, make sure the director or a colleague conducts them. Note examples of accurate and objective recordings that avoid the use of labels. Demonstrate how to rewrite inappropriate recordings so they are accurate and objective. If a staff member needs to repeat activity, provide support and assistance.

Module 12: Program Management (continued)

Learning Activity	What Staff Members Do	What Trainers Do
II. Individualizing the Program	Read about the importance of providing a program that responds to each child as an individual. Review strategies for including children with disabilities. Observe three children (preferably one from each of three age groups) at least once a day for a week. Review observation notes and complete Individualization Summary Forms describing what they learned about each child and how they can build on the children's skills and interests. Discuss the activity with the trainer.	Offer to supervise children while staff practice observing and recording. Help staff analyze their recordings and draw conclusions about children's strengths, interests, and needs. Discuss the completed Individualization Summary Forms. Encourage staff to establish a system for regular observations of all the children.
III. Involving Parents and Children in Program Planning	Read about using parent surveys to collect information about children's interests, skills, and needs. Read about gathering information from children in a variety of ways. Conduct a survey of children in the program to determine their current needs and interests. Use survey results to help children plan and start a club. After the club has met for two weeks, answer questions about what happened. Discuss the activity with colleagues and the trainer.	Discuss using surveys throughout the year to collect information from the children and families in the program. Help staff and children implement club plans. Discuss what took place as the club plans were implemented and what staff might do differently in the future.

Module 12:   Program Management (continued)

Learning Activity	What Staff Members Do	What Trainers Do
IV. Working as a Team for Long-Range and Weekly Planning	Read about the importance of long-range and weekly planning. Review suggested planning categories, how knowledge of individual children guides the planning process, the role of special activities, and evaluation questions used as the last step in the planning process. Review a sample planning form. With a colleague, develop and use a plan for one week. Then answer evaluation questions. Discuss the activity with colleagues and the trainer.	Review and provide feedback on revised weekly plans. Read and discuss responses to the evaluation questions. Discuss how the revised plans meet children's individual needs.
V. Following Administrative Policies and Procedures	Read about administrative policies, practices, and procedures in school-age programs and the types of records they maintain. Review program's administrative policies and procedures for completing various reports. Complete a schedule indicating dates and responsibilities for completing reports.	Discuss schedule for completing records and forms. Help staff schedule time to complete reports.
Summarizing Your Progress	Review recordings from Learning Activity II and answer follow-up questions. Review responses to Pre-Training Assessment, summarize what was learned in this module, and list skills developed or improved.	Discuss summary of progress. Schedule assessments for this module. The Competency Assessment includes observation of a staff meeting.

Strategies for Extending Learning

- Work with staff to review the program's procedures to look for ways to streamline requirements or complete them more efficiently. Help staff plan and conduct a workshop on time-management skills and recordkeeping techniques.

- Introduce staff to a variety of observation and recording formats, such as time sampling, event sampling, rating scales, and skills checklists. Encourage them to pick an instrument or format that serves a particular need—observing to see if the environment is working, noting children's progress in a specific area, keeping records to discuss with parents.

- Provide a videocamera for staff to set up on a tripod in the room or outdoors. Encourage them to let the camera run, cinema-verité style. Then sit with staff and view what the camera has recorded. Discuss what the children did, materials and skills they used, how they interacted with each other and with the staff, and how staff responded.

- Have staff discuss how they can individualize planned activities while including children with a wide range of ages and abilities in that activity. Some examples might include building an obstacle course, planting a garden, or going on a field trip.

Completing Module 13:   Professionalism

Learning Activity	What Staff Members Do	What Trainers Do

Overview and Pre-Training Assessment	Read about what it means to be a professional and about the four stages of professional development.
	
	Read examples of situations in which staff maintained a commitment to professionalism and answer questions.
	
	Respond to questions about their interests and skills and how these relate to working with school-age children. Discuss responses with two colleagues.
	
	Complete Pre-Training Assessment and list three to five skills to improve or topics to learn more about.
	
	Discuss Overview and Pre-Training Assessment with the trainer.
		Review staff members' training files.
		
		Discuss with staff:
		
		    responses to questions;
		
		    examples of times they used their skills and interests at work and children's reactions; and
		
		    Pre-Training Assessment.
		
		Validate where possible from meetings and their knowledge of staff members.

I. Assessing Yourself	Read about standards of quality for school-age programs. Review standards for the outdoor environment as presented in three documents that list standards for quality in school-age programs. Meet with a colleague to discuss and answer questions about how the standards apply to their program and what they can do to improve the outdoor space used by the program. Discuss with the trainer how they can implement their suggestions.	Discuss staff reactions to the standards and how they relate to the program's outdoor environment. Review staff members' suggested improvements to the outdoor space used by the program and help them implement needed changes. Coordinate with the director to order copies of standards if the program has not already done so.

Module 13:   Professionalism (continued)

Learning Activity	What Staff Members Do	What Trainers Do
II. Continuing to Learn About Working with School-Age Children	Read about the many benefits of continued learning, joining professional organizations, and other ways to continue professional growth. Review answers to "Taking a Look at Yourself" in the Overview. Select one item from responses to "I would like to be better at" or "I would like to know more about." Identify resources for learning more about the topic or task. Use information on resources to make short- and long-range plans for professional development, identify possible barriers, and plan ways to overcome them. Discuss the activity with the trainer. Agree on an overall plan to achieve goals.	Provide information about professional organizations, resources, classes, lectures, and conferences staff might like to attend. Help staff build time for training and skill development into their personal schedules. Discuss short- and long-range plans for professional development. Periodically review staff members' progress toward reaching their goals. Help them overcome any barriers to reaching their goals.
III. Applying Professional Ethics at All Times	Review examples of the ethics of school-age care as well as professional and unprofessional behaviors. List examples of how their own professional behavior conforms to the ethics of quality school-age care. Read five ethics case studies and suggest what a school-age professional should do. Use discussion points at the end of module to review the activity with colleagues and the trainer.	Discuss staff members' examples of professional behavior. Point out examples of ethical behavior from their own observations. Continue discussing issues as they arise. Meet with group of staff to discuss responses to case studies. Stress that these are difficult situations and there are no easy answers. Praise all staff members for conscientious work habits and ethical behavior.

Module 13:   Professionalism (continued)

Learning Activity	What Staff Members Do	What Trainers Do
IV. Becoming an Advocate for Children and Families	Read about the importance of advocating for children and families, six ways school-age staff can be advocates, and examples of advocacy opportunities. Develop a plan for becoming an advocate for children and families. Discuss the activity with the trainer.	Discuss current issues related to children and families. Collect articles and bulletins to share with staff. Discuss plans and offer to assist in advocacy efforts. Follow up with information on major issues.
V. Taking Care of Yourself	Read about the importance of taking care of one's physical, emotional, social, and intellectual well-being. Read also about sources of stress and how they might affect a person's well-being. Record what they did to take care of their physical, emotional, social, and intellectual well-being for one day. Review answers and try to do better on following day. Record activities for a second day. Discuss the activity with the trainer. Write a brief plan for taking care of oneself.	Reinforce the importance of taking care of one's physical, emotional, intellectual, and social well-being. Review plans and offer to assist in implementing them. Be a good model by taking care of yourself.
Summarizing Your Progress	Review responses to Pre-Training Assessment, summarize what was learned in this module, and list skills developed or improved.	Discuss summary of progress. Schedule Knowledge Assessment for this module. There is no Competency Assessment as the skills used are not readily observable.

Strategies for Extending Learning

- Hold a discussion about current issues affecting children and families in the community or state, and discuss ways in which staff can become more involved in advocacy efforts.

- Build a comprehensive lending library of professional books, journals, and audiovisual materials on school-age care.

- Share information about classes on stress management, nutrition, assertiveness, and other topics relevant to a healthy lifestyle.

- Encourage staff members to be partners in each other's professional development. They might share rides, care for each other's children at night or on the weekends, plan and lead workshops together, share resources, and otherwise help each other reach professional goals.

- Discuss with staff member the next steps in their professional development—for example, a school-age credential, college courses, or continued self-study. Help them understand how these modules fit into their ongoing professional growth.

III. Leading Group Training Sessions

III. Leading Group Training Sessions

This chapter describes:

- settings for group training;

- selecting training techniques;

- attending to logistics;

- encouraging staff to be active participants;

- evaluating training; and

- a sample training outline for Module 10, Guidance.

Settings for Group Training

Although *Caring for Children in School-Age Programs* is designed to be implemented as a supervised, self-instructional training program, it can also serve as the focus for a series of workshops or as a textbook for college courses. School-age programs could use the modules as an in-house training program and discuss Learning Activities at staff meetings or at scheduled professional development sessions.

The chart that follows illustrates how the 13 modules in *Caring for Children in School-Age Programs* might be organized into college courses. This model is based on 12 credit hours that would meet the requirements for college credit. Another way that colleges might award credit is to offer a series of one-credit-hour classes based on the modules, thus giving staff a range of choices for augmenting their training experiences.

Course Title	Modules Covered	Suggested Clock Hours
Establishing the Environment	Safe Healthy Program Environment	12 12 14
Child Growth and Development: Cognitive and Physical	Physical Cognitive Communication Creative	10 10 10 10
Child Growth and Development: Social and Emotional	Self Social Guidance	11 11 16
Introduction to the Profession	Families Program Management Professionalism	10 20 10
Applied School-Age Practices (Lab or Practicum)	This course would include observation of a student's application of material presented in class and individualized support and feedback.	16

When using the modules for courses or group training sessions, it is important to include observation visits of staff working in a school-age program as a component of the training. Your group meetings will provide valuable information about each staff member's progress; however, it is crucial to also offer individualized, on-site support that is based on systematic, objective observations.

If you teach a college course, observation visits can be established as a lab or practicum. Thirteen observation visits are considered ideal (one per module). A minimum of eight is recommended when using these materials as the core curriculum for the courses listed in the chart on the previous page. For each course, one visit can be used to provide support and feedback and one can be used to administer the assessments.

In planning training based on *Caring for Children in School-Age Programs*—or on any subject, for that matter—it's important to reflect on what we know about how adults learn and to use care in selecting training techniques that meet individual and group needs.

Selecting Training Techniques

To a large extent, your choice of training techniques depends on your personal preferences and philosophy of training. For example, if you're a skilled lecturer, you will want to include mini-lectures as part of your workshops. On the other hand, if you're uncomfortable as a lecturer, you may rely on group-oriented activities. Your choice of techniques will also reflect the preferences of those whom you are training. This means you should select techniques that suit your style and use a variety of approaches to meet the different learning styles of the people you'll be training.

Plan a balance of different types of activities using a variety of instructional media. A balance of approaches contributes to the group's interest and ultimately ensures greater retention and application of skills and content. To encourage participants' active involvement, use role playing, small group analysis, discussion, and case studies. These techniques allow participants to apply training concepts, principles, and strategies to real-life situations.

The training techniques listed here represent a potpourri of ideas. Some will be perfect for you; others will not. Try out as many methods as possible to find those that suit you. Nearly all these techniques can be modified and reshaped to accommodate both your needs and the needs of the staff attending training.

Written Handouts

Written material such as articles from professional journals or chapters in textbooks can be used as background reading or to provide further illustration of topics addressed in the Learning Activities. You can also use written materials to summarize content presented, as training assignments, or as supplemental readings for interested participants.

Audiovisuals

Audiovisuals can be very effective training tools. Videotapes can show realistic and relevant scenes from school-age programs. Your own slides or videotapes of programs would also be a good way to illustrate some of the ideas covered in training.

Overhead Transparencies

Overhead transparencies are recommended as accompaniments to presentations. They not only break up the monotony of the spoken voice but also reinforce the key points of a lecture for participants. Here are some suggestions for developing transparencies.

- Include key words and phrases only.
- Use large printed letters that can be read from any point in the room.
- Keep illustrations or graphs simple.
- Ensure sufficient contrast between the background color and lettering so overheads are easy to read.

Problem-Solving Activities

One of the most popular—and effective—training techniques is group problem-solving. Brainstorming solutions to realistic problems energizes a group and generates many creative ideas. The theory behind brainstorming is to separate idea creation from idea evaluation. This strategy works best in groups of 5 to 12 and requires a recorder and a moderator. Here are the rules for brainstorming:

- All ideas are listed; no critical remarks are allowed.
- "Hitchhiking" is allowed—if one participant can improve upon or combine previously mentioned ideas, so much the better.
- "Freewheeling" is encouraged—even outlandish ideas keep the group momentum going.
- The more the better—the more ideas generated, the more likely there will be some viable solutions among these ideas.
- Evaluation comes only after all ideas have been generated.

Brainstorming can be used to suggest answers to questions such as the following:

- How can we involve more parents in the school-age program?
- What activities appeal to multi-age groups of children?
- What materials and activities do we need to implement a new club?
- Which community agencies and businesses could be partners with the program?

Some other problem-solving techniques you might wish to try are described below.

- **Reverse brainstorming**—participants identify all the negative aspects of a problem that needs to be remedied. This can be especially useful in examining current practices to see what isn't working, such as why children are getting into fights in one of the interest areas.

- The **slip method**—participants write their solutions to a stated problem on slips of paper that are collected and grouped into logical categories for analysis and discussion. This can be especially useful in finding plausible solutions to a specific problem, such as how to help the older children create their own special place.

- The **Delphi technique (group approach)**—participants generate as many responses to a particular problem as they can. Ideas are consolidated and presented for the group to consider and rank in order of viability. The filtering process identifies three to five "best" solutions to a particular problem.

Case Studies

An important advantage of the case study method is that it helps participants apply what has been taught through lectures or assigned reading to real-life examples. By providing illustrative stories, case studies can be powerful tools for helping participants apply theory to the real world. Many of the vignettes and examples in the modules could be used to develop case studies.

When using case studies, distribute a copy to each participant. Ask them to read the case, then discuss it in pairs, in small groups, or as the full group. Ask questions such as the following to stimulate thinking:

- What went wrong?
- What worked well?
- How could this problem be avoided in the future?
- How could this individual build on his or her success?
- What did the children learn from this experience?
- What feedback would you provide to this individual?

Role Plays

Putting oneself in another person's shoes allows participants to act out real-life situations in a risk-free environment. By seeing things from another perspective, participants gain insight into various ways to approach a problem issue. Keep in mind that some adults are very uncomfortable during role plays and may prefer to watch. Pressuring them to join in—"Oh come on, you'll have a good time"—generally backfires for both trainer and participant.

Discussion Techniques

The fishbowl, fantasy, and visualization techniques are used by trainers to stimulate discussion. For the **fishbowl**, divide participants into two groups, forming an inner and an outer ring of a circle. Participants in the inner group receive an assignment based on content presented in the training. For example, the inner group might consider how staff can enhance their professional image. While the inner group discusses this problem for five to ten minutes, outer group members observe the discussion. At the end of the allotted time, the two groups switch roles. At the conclusion of the second discussion, both groups comment on what they've seen and heard. Quite often, the discussion quickly becomes analytical because of mutual observations. This technique also stimulates discussion among participants who are initially shy about contributing.

Fantasy and visualization are techniques used to draw on right brain (creative thinking) powers. **Fantasy** techniques most commonly involve asking participants to reflect on "what if…" situations. For example, you might say, "What if you had unlimited financial resources. How would you equip the school-age program?" This type of exercise allows participants to come up with the components of an ideal inventory. They can then compare the ideal to reality and see where compromises are appropriate. Conversely, you can also use fantasy to think through worst-case scenarios.

Visualization helps participants relate the tasks at hand to past experiences. For example, you might ask participants to think about an experience in which they were forced to do something that made them uncomfortable. What were the circumstances? How did they feel? What did they do to relieve their discomfort? Did they ever get over being uncomfortable? You might use this type of reflection if you sense that participants are uncomfortable dealing with particular situations, such as having to communicate unpopular information to parents.

Mini-lectures

These are shorter versions of lectures or oral presentations. A straight verbal presentation is useful when you need to cover a large amount of basic material quickly. It can provide everyone in the group with the same framework or background material as a starting point. Try to limit use of this technique to 20 minutes at a time.

It is important to provide a handout summarizing the main points and to let participants know it is available. Use visuals to illustrate key concepts. This supports the research which says we retain 50 percent of what we see and hear compared to 20 percent of what we only hear.

At the close of the mini-lecture, review your key points, ask the group to summarize, conduct a discussion of the main points, or plan an activity which relates to the material covered. This allows participants to assimilate and make the material their own—to relate it to their own thinking, decide what it means to them, and consider how it affects them on the job.

Group Discussions

Small groups are used to facilitate discussion and idea sharing. They are a particularly good way of encouraging shy participants to share their ideas. They offer more intimate connections among group members. The optimal size for small groups is three to six. Small groups encourage more active involvement from all participants and help them build networks and relationships.

To divide into small groups, try one of these methods:

- Ask participants to sort themselves into groups of a specified size.
- Count off by a specified number.
- Distribute cards with pictures, stickers, or numbers; have participants match cards and group accordingly.
- Assign participants to groups according to roles or ability combinations.

- Distribute single parts of four to six piece puzzles—participants form groups by assembling the puzzles.

- Place pictures or names of objects that can be classified into a bag (for example, furniture, clothing, animals). Have participants choose a card then form a group with others whose objects fit in the same category.

Here are some suggestions for using small groups effectively:

- Be sure participants sit in a close circle as far as possible from other groups.

- Give three- and one-minute warnings before ending discussions.

- Ask groups to report back to the whole group by presenting one or two ideas. Go from group to group until all new ideas are listed. This prevents repetitious reporting, and the first group to report doesn't "use up" all the popular answers.

- Reassemble as a full group without sharing what was discussed in the small groups. Reporting may not always be necessary, and not sharing discussions supports each small group's sense of uniqueness. You could suggest the groups share informally, perhaps during the break.

Large group discussions can be used to break up a mini-lecture, discuss reactions to a videotape, and give participants an opportunity to contribute to and learn from their peers. If an entire group is 15 people or less, discussions involving the whole group allow members to contribute to and hear all the ideas presented.

The trainer's role is to facilitate communication and make sure messages are sent, received, and understood. It is important to receive participants' comments without judgment. If a statement indicates a lack of understanding, use the next break to discuss it with the participant. If a statement is incorrect, provide the correct information as diplomatically as possible, "Many people think that is true; however, the state health office recommends . . ."

During large group discussions some participants might become frustrated because they feel ignored, misunderstood, or unable to participate. You need to observe both the behavior of the group as a whole and that of specific individuals. When a participant's comments have apparently been misunderstood, paraphrase and clarify them for the whole group. "I think Trinh was saying that . . ."

Attending to Logistics

No matter what the topic, training is most successful when it is well planned. What may seem like simple details can enhance or destroy a training session. Attention to logistics is worth the time you invest. Here are some general pointers for making logistical arrangements that support comfortable and productive training sessions.

- Schedule sessions at times that are convenient for staff—for example, after the children leave for school in the morning, or, if applicable, on in-service days. School-age staff have steady demands on their professional and personal time. Accommodating to their schedules is courteous, and it increases the possibility of high attendance.

- Notify participants of the date, time, and location of the training. If appropriate, provide directions for finding the building and room where the session will be held. Provide an agenda and other preparatory materials in advance.

- Provide refreshments. By letting participants know in advance that food and drink are available, you eliminate another deterrent to attendance. A snack break will refresh minds and energize participants.

- Visit the training site to make sure the chairs provide enough support so that participants can sit for a long period of time without getting restless. Check also to be sure there are tables on which participants can place their belongings and write.

- Prepare or arrange for all needed materials and equipment in advance. This includes audiovisual equipment, videos, flip charts, markers, tape, chalk, handouts, and evaluation forms. Check to make sure the equipment works and that there are replacement bulbs, extension cords, and adapters on hand.

- Arrange furniture in a pattern that suits your training style. Many trainers prefer circles, semi-circles, or small tables because they encourage participant discussions. As a general rule, training is best received when the room is informally arranged.

- Check to be sure the room temperature is comfortable prior to the start of the session. The temperature should be neither too hot not too cold, and air should be circulating freely. An overheated room can put an audience to sleep more quickly than a boring speaker.

- Display name tags, sign-in sheets, agendas, and reference materials in areas that are readily accessible to participants.

By attending to these few logistical concerns, you'll be able to focus on the content of the training—rather than searching for extension cords or a building engineer to turn up the heat. Preparation goes a long way when it comes to training.

Encouraging Staff to Be Active Participants

For some staff, participating in group training sessions will be a new experience. Even an experienced staff member may feel shy about talking aloud in a group, sharing experiences and ideas, or asking questions. As a trainer, one of your most important functions is to help participants feel comfortable about expressing their ideas. Here are some ideas you might try to help staff feel comfortable enough to actively participate in and benefit from training.

At the Start of the Session

- **Greet participants at the door.** Welcome them to the session.

- **Discuss the rules and guidelines.** If, for example, smoking is prohibited in the training room, participants should be advised about areas where smoking is permitted during breaks.

- **Point out the location of rest rooms, telephones, and water fountains.** This will minimize interruptions once training starts.

- **Provide an overview of the session.** Explain the goals and objectives, describe the content and activities, and refer to the handouts. Training is more effective when the group understands and shares a commitment to the goals and objectives.

- **Let participants know they are responsible for their own learning.** Explain that everyone will take something different from the session, depending on what is important to them, how much effort they put into the session, and whether they integrate and use what they learn.

- **Underscore the importance of training.** Stress that the purpose of training is to help staff do their jobs better and to enhance their professional development.

During Discussions

- **Encourage participants to use active listening and to express their opinions.** Acknowledge that sharing ideas and experiences in a group may feel a little uncomfortable at first. Emphasize that everyone's views are valuable and there is usually more than one way to approach a topic. Do not embarrass participants by forcing each person to contribute.

- **Look for "body-language" cues.** They may alert you to someone's discomfort with the subject matter being discussed (squirming), shyness about contributing (eye avoidance), or anger (turning away with the entire body). Then try to respond to what you see.

- **Guide participants to reach a compromise or at least respect conflicting points of view.** This is particularly important when conflicts or disagreements occur.

- **Invite participants to ask questions.** Questions help you explain information and eliminate misunderstandings. Before responding, rephrase the question to clarify what is being asked. Redirect some questions to the group to help participants find answers based on their own experiences and expertise. If you can't answer a question, admit it and try to find the answer later.

- **Ask questions in response to cues from the audience.** At times, it is appropriate to use both direct questions ("What books do you think would be helpful to a child whose parents are divorcing?") and open-ended questions ("How would you handle that situation?"). Also, refer a question to the entire group if you sense that an in-depth discussion would be beneficial. ("That's a tough problem. Does anyone have a suggestion?")

Throughout the Session

- **Draw on participants' experiences.** Training is more meaningful when participants can relate concepts to personal situations and experiences.

- **Emphasize skill development rather than rote learning of "correct" responses.** Learning is the process of assimilating new information and using it to improve skills.

- **Encourage participants to make interpretations and draw conclusions.** Effective training provides background information, data, and examples participants can use to identify patterns or trends, make generalizations, and draw conclusions.

- **Adjust the agenda to meet the needs of participants.** Use a mixture of planned and spontaneous activities and content.

- **Use small group activities to discuss feelings.** Consider using role playing, simulations, or problem-solving assignments.

- **Summarize what has been said and done.** Take time to review as you move from one segment of the training to the next and at the end of the session.

- **Be available during breaks to discuss issues and topics.** Some participants may be more comfortable sharing their views with you one-on-one rather than in front of the whole group.

Evaluating Training

As a trainer you need to know whether you've met your training goals. Did the participants increase their understanding of the content? Do they feel capable of implementing what they have learned? Do they think the training session was beneficial? Did they gain skills or change attitudes?

To answer these questions you can use group or individual training evaluations. If participants are not learning and gaining new skills, you'll want to adjust your training as rapidly as possible to address the pinpointed weaknesses.

The following are two examples of evaluation techniques that involve the whole group in offering feedback.

Pluses and Wishes. On chart paper or a blackboard draw a chart with two columns. Label one "pluses" and the other "wishes." You can ask a volunteer to record participants' responses. Ask, "What did you like about this training—what were the pluses?" and "What do you wish the training had included but did not?" Responses are likely to vary from concerns about logistics, "The chairs were uncomfortable," to comments on the content, "I can use the ideas for no-prop activities immediately."

Gets/Wants Chart—On chart paper or a blackboard make a chart with four quadrants, like the axes on a graph. Label as in the following example.

Got—Wanted	Didn't Get—Wanted
Suggestions for guiding behavior *Opportunities to learn from other staff*	*Tips for handling swearing* *Refreshments*
Got—Didn't Want	**Didn't Get—Didn't Want**
Video I'd seen before *Role plays*	

As you go through each quadrant ask participants to provide examples of parts of the training they "got, and wanted," "got, but didn't want," and "didn't get, and wanted." When you get to the last quadrant explain that this one doesn't need to be addressed because the items must be irrelevant to their jobs ("You didn't get this information and it doesn't matter because you didn't want it!"). See the chart above for examples of the types of responses participants might offer. When planning future training, you can review the responses and decide if you should continue to offer the things they "got and wanted," provide things they "didn't get and wanted," and eliminate the things they "got and didn't want!"

Individual questionnaires, completed at the end of the training or returned one or two weeks later, can help you assess which parts of the training were well received. (An example of a training questionnaire appears on the next page.) For example, did participants like group exercises but dislike the mini-lectures? Did they think too much content was presented in too short a time? By reviewing participants' reactions, you can answer questions such as these:

- How effectively did the training accomplish its objectives?

- How relevant was the training to the participants' jobs?

- What changes to the training are needed?

- Do participants need more in-depth training? On what topics?

Participant evaluations are a valuable tool for assessing whether training needs have been met. As you review the results, though, bear in mind that not everyone is always going to be satisfied with training. Some variations in answers are to be expected, and you should revise your approach only if warranted.

Training Evaluation

Session Title: _____   **Date:** _____

Trainer: _____

	Completely	Somewhat	Not At All

A. Content

1. Did the topics address your needs? _____ _____ _____

2. Was the information relevant to your job? _____ _____ _____

B. Trainer

3. Was the trainer well-informed on the subject? _____ _____ _____

4. Did the trainer help you learn? _____ _____ _____

5. Was the presentation well-organized? _____ _____ _____

C. Materials

6. How appropriate and usable were the handouts? _____ _____ _____

7. How appropriate were other resources such as videos? _____ _____ _____

D. Suggestions or Comments (Indicate your likes, dislikes, and recommendations.)

E. How do you plan to apply what you learned in this training?

Your name (optional): _____

Sample Training Outline for Module 10: Guidance

Organizing training sessions in advance will help you be a more effective trainer. As you plan group sessions based on any of the modules in *Caring for Children in School-Age Programs*, think about the training techniques you will use. For example, in the outline that follows, you could use brainstorming for the Discussion Questions and role play staff observations during Review of Activity. You can use the following outline for group training on Module 10, adapting the suggestions to address individual interests and training needs. Ask participants to submit their completed activities for your review and written comments prior to the training session (you may need to develop a system for doing this). Explain that you will return the activities, with your comments, at the end of each session. Staff members who would like to discuss your feedback can meet with you individually.

Overview

I. Opening

Begin with an open-ended question such as:

- What does the word "discipline" mean to you?

- How do you handle discipline at your program?

- What are some difficulties you experience in guiding children's behavior?

- What does your discipline policy tell parents?

II. Discussion Questions

- How do children use self-discipline?
    - To make decisions for themselves.
    - To solve their own problems.
    - To correct their mistakes.
    - To do what is right without someone telling them what to do.
    - To take responsibility for their own actions.
    - To learn the rules for living in our society.

- What are some of the reasons children misbehave?
    - They want to test the limits set by adults.
    - The program's schedule doesn't meet their needs.
    - The rules at home or at school are different from those at the program.
    - A school or family situation is upsetting them.
    - They need attention but don't know how to ask for it.
    - They miss their parents.
    - They are tired, hungry, or ill.
    - They feel afraid or insecure.
    - They want to do things for themselves.

III. Discussion of Overview

A. Review the examples of ways staff demonstrate their competence in guiding children's behavior. Ask staff to give examples showing how they use their skills in each category.

- How does your environment encourage self-discipline?

- What positive methods do you use to guide children?

- How do you help children understand and express their feelings in acceptable ways?

B. Discuss the vignettes and responses to the questions.

- How do you feel about the way the staff member handled this situation?

- How would you handle a similar situation in your program?

C. Discuss the section on Your Own Self-Discipline.

- How does self-discipline affect your own behavior?
  - It guides my behavior at work, at home, and in society.
  - It helps me feel good about myself.
  - It lets me respond automatically because I have learned and accepted certain rules of behavior and want to avoid certain consequences.

- How does your self-discipline affect your work with children?
  - Modeling self-discipline helps children learn acceptable ways to behave.
  - Being in control of one's behavior leads to higher self-esteem, which may make me more effective and skilled.

IV. Ending the Session

Answer questions. Return staff members' completed Overviews and Pre-Training Assessments. Schedule times to meet individually with staff to discuss their responses and the three to five skills and topics they want to learn more about.

Learning Activity I: Using Your Knowledge of Child Development to Guide Behavior

---

I. Opening

Ask staff for examples of the techniques they use to guide the behavior of children of different ages.

II. Discussion Questions

- How can knowledge of child development help you guide behavior?
  - I will have more realistic expectations of children's abilities.
  - I can provide guidance that reflects developmental characteristics.

- Why is it important to consider Kohlberg's stages of moral development?
  - Children at different stages have different reasons for behaving and following rules.
  - Staff can tailor their explanations of why rules are needed to reflect children's moral reasoning.

III. Review of Activity

Ask staff the ages of the children in their program. Focus your discussion on the ages with the highest representation, but be sure to spend some time on each age group. Encourage staff to give examples from their own experiences, as noted on the charts they completed in the Learning Activity. When appropriate, offer examples from your own observations of how school-age staff guide the behavior of a multi-age group. The following examples of appropriate responses are organized by age group; however, some also would be appropriate for children younger or older than the age listed.

- What can you do to guide **5-to-7-year old** children's behavior?
  - Encourage children to use thinking skills to solve their disagreements.
  - Provide duplicates of popular items and materials.
  - Encourage small group activities.
  - Play games with children so they can learn the rules.
  - Allow children to do as much as possible for themselves.
  - Be available when children are ready to share their feelings.

- What can you do to guide **8-to-10-year old** children's behavior?
  - Teach children to use conflict resolution techniques.
  - Ask children to explain the rules for made-up games.
  - Encourage children to make amends for their actions.
  - Provide outlets for reducing stress such as soft music and earphones.
  - Compliment children when they use good judgment.
  - Include opportunities for children to make choices, form clubs, and lead meetings.

- What can you do to guide **11-to-12 year old** children's behavior?
  - Teach children how to present and support their opinions.
  - Help children accept the consequences for breaking program rules.
  - Give children responsibility so they feel grown up and independent.
  - Make sure equipment is sized appropriately for older children.
  - Encourage children to review their plans before carrying them out.
  - Discuss ways to respond to peers who want them to do something they know is not allowed.

IV. Additional Resources/Activities

Provide posterboard and markers so staff can make charts similar to those in this chapter. Post them in an area used by staff so they can add additional examples of what children are like and how they used this information to promote self-discipline.

V. Ending the Session

A. Give a brief overview of the next Learning Activity.

B. Ask staff to draw plans of their indoor and outdoor environments, labeling features that promote children's self-discipline, and bring the plans to the next meeting. If possible, staff could also bring photographs of the indoor and outdoor areas used by the program.

C. Return staff members' completed activities with your comments. Offer to review and discuss these during individual meetings with interested staff.

Learning Activity II: Creating an Environment that Supports Self-Discipline

---

I. Opening

Ask staff to share the plans and/or photographs of their program's physical environments and discuss how different features promote self-discipline. Point out features such as the following and the positive behaviors they promote:

Feature of Environment	Positive Behavior
There are individual cubbies.	Children store their belongings, recognize items in cubbies are off limits, and learn to take care of personal and program materials.
The daily schedule is posted at eye level.	Children get involved in activities. They feel secure because they know what's going on at the program.
Cleaning supplies are stored within children's reach.	Children clean up after themselves.
Materials used together are stored together.	Clean-up time goes smoothly as children know where things are stored.
Materials are stored where children can reach them.	Children make independent choices without waiting for staff to get out things they want to use.
There are comfortable places to sit and read or talk with a friend.	Children relax, take a break, relieve stress, or get away from the group for a while.
There are clearly defined spaces for different activities and clear traffic patterns.	Children stay out of each other's way; they play and work without interruption.
The environment can be rearranged to reflect changes in children's skills, needs, and interests.	Children become interested and involved in the new and different materials and activities.
The outdoor area supports a variety of activities.	Children are energized by going outdoors and using their physical skills.

II. Discussion Questions

- How can staff create a social environment that encourages self-discipline?
  - Involve children in making decisions about the program.
  - Notice and provide for children's interests.
  - Use a normal tone and volume when speaking to children.
  - Let children know they value cooperation.
  - Offer children meaningful ways to participate in daily routines.
  - Involve children when setting rules.
  - Encourage children to help each other.
  - Teach children cooperative games and minimize competition in general.

- What questions should staff ask when problem behaviors occur again and again?
  - When do problems occur?
  - In what areas of the environment do problems surface?
  - Which children are involved?
  - What are the children usually doing?

III. Review of Activity

A. Ask staff to share their responses to Creating an Environment That Promotes Self-Discipline, and compare them to those provided at the end of the module.

B. Discuss problem behaviors encountered by staff and how rearranging the environment or changing the social climate might eliminate them.

C. Encourage staff to help each other develop solutions.

IV. Additional Resources/Activities

A. Bring slides you have collected illustrating arrangements of furniture and materials that promote self-discipline.

B. Encourage staff to visit each other's rooms and share ideas.

V. Ending the Session

A. Give a brief overview of the next Learning Activity.

B. Ask staff if they have (or have access to) tape players. Suggest that they tape themselves interacting with children.

C. Return staff members' completed activities with your comments. Offer to review and discuss these during individual meetings with interested staff.

Learning Activity III: Guiding Children's Behavior

I. Opening

Begin this session by having staff think about the differences between discipline and punishment.

- Discipline means guiding and directing children to help them learn acceptable behavior. Discipline helps children learn what they can and cannot do.

- Punishment means controlling children through fear. It may stop children's negative behavior for the moment, but does not help children gain inner controls.

II. Discussion Questions

- What might children be expressing through their behaviors?
  - I feel lonely because . . .
  - I am angry because . . .
  - I am afraid the other children will laugh at me.
  - I want my work to be perfect.
  - I need some limits.
  - I can't do what you asked me to do.

- What are some positive guidance approaches that help school-age children develop self-discipline? (Ask for examples of approaches staff have used.)
  - Help children use problem solving skills to develop solutions.
  - Talk with children privately, away from the group.

- Use a pre-arranged signal to remind a child to use self-control.
- Focus on the behavior, not the child.
- Help children understand the consequences of their behavior and help them make amends.
- Assume the role of authority only when necessary—but do so firmly.
- Gain control of your own angry feelings before disciplining a child.
- Intervene in children's conflicts only when necessary to prevent injuries.

III. Review of Activity

A. Have staff work in pairs or small groups to share their responses to the situations in the Learning Activity.

- What else might be learned from the observation notes on this child?

- What other positive guidance strategies might help this child develop self-discipline?

B. Ask each pair or group to present what they learned from one another. Discuss any questions or areas of disagreement that came up.

IV. Additional Resources/Activities

A. If staff have brought tape recordings of their conversations with children, invite volunteers to share their examples with the group. Lead a discussion pointing out positive interactions you heard.

B. Give sample situations where staff would need to step in and guide children's behavior. Have the group identify strategies that would be age appropriate and encourage self-discipline.

V. Ending the Session

A. Give a brief overview of the next Learning Activity.

B. Return staff members' completed activities with your comments. Offer to review and discuss these during individual meetings with interested staff.

Learning Activity IV: Teaching Children to Use Conflict Resolution Techniques

---

I. Opening

Ask staff to share examples of the kinds of conflicts they experience in life and the strategies they use to resolve conflicts within their families, with friends, or with colleagues. Point out the following:

- conflicts are a part of life; and

- when handled effectively, conflicts can be productive and lead to better communication.

II. Discussion Questions

- What are some typical conflicts that arise in your program?

- Are the conflicts related to disagreements about resources? about needs? about values?

- What can you do to minimize the sources of disagreements?
  - Work with children to set up a system for taking turns.
  - Order more of popular materials.
  - Identify and respond to children's needs.
  - Teach children to express their views politely, without putting each other down.

- What are some characteristics of school-age programs that reduce conflicts? How does your program atmosphere reduce conflicts?
  - There is a cooperative atmosphere.
  - Staff and children demonstrate tolerance.
  - Staff and children have good communication skills.
  - Staff and children express feelings and emotions appropriately.
  - Staff have appropriate expectations for children's behavior.
  - Staff and children use conflict resolution to discuss and resolve disagreements.

- Which of the conflict resolution techniques described in this activity are or could be effective in your program?

- Why is it important to teach school-age children conflict resolution skills?
  - Children are developmentally ready to learn and use conflict resolution.
  - Children will learn to consider the views and feelings of others.
  - Children can use these skills throughout their lives in a variety of situations.
  - Children feel more independent when they can solve their own problems.
  - The program is a more peaceful, pleasant place when conflicts are resolved.

III. Review of Activity

A. Ask each staff member to describe the conflict that took place in his or her program. After the description, ask the other participants which technique they would recommend for the situation. Then have the staff member discuss the technique actually used and how it helped to resolve the conflict.

B. If the conflict resolution technique used by a staff member was not effective, involve the group in analyzing the situation.
  - Which children were involved?
  - What are their ages?
  - What are they like?
  - Did the technique fit the children's ages and skill levels?
  - Did the technique fit the conflict?
  - What techniques might have been more effective? Why?

IV. Additional Resources/Activities

Provide a copy of the resource referenced in this Learning Activity, *Creative Conflict Resolution* by William Kreidler as well as other resources that describe conflict resolution techniques and how to teach children to use them.

V. Ending the Session

A. Give a brief overview of the next Learning Activity.

B. Ask staff to bring copies of their program's rules and limits to the next session.

C. Return staff members' completed activities with your comments. Offer to review and discuss these during individual meetings with interested staff.

Learning Activity V: Setting Rules and Limits

I. Opening

Ask staff members to share one rule in place in their program. List each rule on chart paper. Then ask:

- How do these rules work for you?
- How do you know when a rule is or is not working?
- How frequently are rules updated?
- How are children involved in setting rules?
- How do you help children appreciate the reasons for the rules?

II. Discussion Questions

- Why is it important for school-age programs to have rules and limits?
    - Rules and limits help adults and children agree on behaviors that are acceptable and those that are not.
    - When they know adults will enforce rules and limits consistently, children feel freer to explore and experiment.

- Why is it important to involve children in creating rules?
    - Children are more likely to respect rules they helped to create.
    - Children are more likely to understand the reasons why rules are needed if they discussed and helped set the rules.

- Why is it important to have just enough rules?
    - When there are too many rules children can't remember them.
    - When there are too few rules the environment might be unsafe or disorderly.

- Why might you need to have different rules for different age groups?
    - Rules should reflect children's abilities and stages of development.
    - Rules should reflect children's increasing maturity and their ability to handle more freedom and responsibility.

III. Review of Activity

A. Have staff turn the rules they listed in this activity into positive statements that remind children of what to do.

B. Ask for volunteers to share the examples of Rules for the School-Age Program, and their responses to the questions on page 228 of Volume II. Stress the importance of respecting and acknowledging children's feelings.

IV. Additional Resources/Activities

Ask staff to work in pairs to share and discuss their copies of the rules in place in their program. Have the pairs rewrite rules as needed to make them positive statements and to identify rules that might not be necessary or might need revisions to reflect children's growth and maturity.

V. Ending the Session

A. Give a brief overview of the next Learning Activity and Summarizing Your Progress at the end of the module.

B. Return staff members' completed activities with your comments. Offer to review and discuss these during individual meetings with interested staff.

Learning Activity VI: Responding to Challenging Behaviors and Summarizing Your Progress

---

I. Opening

Ask staff:

- Why do we use the term "challenging behavior" instead of "bad behavior" or "problem child"?

- How do you handle talking back, kicking, swearing, temper tantrums, and so on?

- Have you tried any of the suggestions in the Learning Activity?

II. Discussion Questions

- What challenging behaviors have you encountered?

- What were the children trying to express through their behavior?

- Have you identified any of the listed causes of challenging behaviors?
    - a child who needs more attention than he or she is getting
    - a child who is affected by a physical condition
    - a child who is feeling bored or confined
    - a child who is seeking more control of the situation

- If so, how did you respond to each child?

III. Review of Activity

Ask for volunteers to discuss the child on whom they focused in the Learning Activity, and the plan they developed with the parents to address the challenging behavior. To maintain confidentiality, staff should not use the child's name. Focus on the process used to find out what was causing the challenging behavior.

IV. Additional Resources/Activities

Invite a mental health specialist to your session to share examples of strategies for helping children overcome challenging behaviors.

V. Summarizing Your Progress

A. Ask staff to share one item from their summary of what they learned while working on this module.

B. Ask staff to share some of the ways they adapted or changed their approach to discipline. How have children reacted? How have parents responded to the revised strategies?

VI. Ending the Session

A. Return staff members' completed activities and summary of progress with your comments. Offer to review and discuss these during individual meetings with interested staff.

B. Meet individually with staff to set up times to administer the Knowledge and Competency Assessments.

If you wish to plan group training sessions using other modules in *Caring for Children in School-Age Programs*, you can use the Planning Form for Group Sessions in Appendix A.

IV. Assessing Each Staff Member's Progress

IV. Assessing Each Staff Member's Progress

This chapter includes:

- guidance on administering the knowledge assessments;
- guidance on conducting the competency assessments;
- strategies for discussing assessment results;
- knowledge assessments for all modules; and
- competency assessments for Modules 1 through 12.

Trainers administer the assessments after staff members have successfully completed all parts of a module—the Overview and Pre-Training Assessment, the Learning Activities, and Summarizing Your Progress. The Knowledge Assessments validate a staff member's understanding of the information presented in the module; the Competency Assessments allow the individual to demonstrate competence by using applicable skills while working with children.

After discussing the staff member's responses to Summarizing Your Progress, provide a copy of the Competency Assessment criteria for the module (included in this chapter after the Knowledge Assessments). Review these criteria with the staff member and decide whether he or she is ready for assessment. (Having provided feedback on all the Learning Activities, you will already have a good idea whether the staff member is ready.) If a staff member is not ready for assessment, suggest repeating one or more Learning Activity or reviewing additional training resources. If the decision is to go ahead with the Knowledge and Competency Assessments, schedule a convenient time to administer them.

The assessment process is designed as one more step in the learning process. If necessary, try to alleviate the staff member's test anxiety. Explain that he or she will continue to receive support if performance on either assessment is not successful. Reassure the individual that there will be continued opportunities to develop the necessary competencies.

Trainers will need to maintain a supply of the assessments; therefore, it might be helpful to set up a filing system for storing copies of the assessments and answer sheets.

Administering the Knowledge Assessments

The Knowledge Assessments are paper-and-pencil exercises that test the staff member's knowledge of the information and concepts presented in the module. The questions are in multiple-choice, matching, short-answer, and true/false formats. They are based on the Overview and Learning Activities. Most staff members will need approximately 20 to 30 minutes of uninterrupted time to complete the Knowledge Assessment. The Knowledge Assessment can be administered before or after the Competency Assessment.

For some staff, it may have been a long a time since they have taken a test. Remind them to read each question completely before attempting to answer it. Also, suggest that they go back and review all of their answers before turning in the assessment. This should help them catch mistakes made because they wrote on the wrong line or misread a question.

Conducting Competency Assessments

Competency Assessments are scheduled times when trainers complete written observations of the staff member working with children. They then use their notes from this observation—and others conducted during the past month—to determine whether the staff member has demonstrated competence. Modules 1 through 12 include both Knowledge and Competency Assessments. Module 13 has a Knowledge Assessment only since mastery of the skills developed through this module cannot be readily determined during an observation period.

Staff members receive their copy of the Competency Assessment criteria during the feedback conference for Summarizing Your Progress. Trainers use the same criteria to determine successful completion of a module. The criteria are drawn from the Pre-Training Assessment and address the skills covered in the module. Most of the behaviors are observable and measurable.

Trainers can conduct the Competency Assessment observation in the morning or afternoon, depending on the day's activities and the skills being observed, and provide feedback on both assessments immediately or the next day.

Appendix C contains trainer observation forms for the Competency Assessments. The forms for each module include two pages for notes, followed by a list of assessment criteria. There are spaces to indicate whether each criteria has been met, partially met, or not met.

The Competency Assessments for Modules 1, 2, 3, 10, and 11 begin with several items related to the environment and procedures. Trainers assess these criteria by reviewing documentation, looking at the environment, and questioning the staff member. They should be assessed immediately prior to the observation period.

The recommended observation period is one hour, but this may vary depending on the time of the day, what the children are doing, and the scheduled and unscheduled activities that take place. You may want to observe at a particular time of day so you can witness a specific routine or activity (for example, you might want to observe the morning departure for school or outdoor play). For several modules the Competency Assessment should be conducted at a specific time: Module 1, Safe should include an emergency drill; Module 11, Families, should be conducted during either drop-off or pick-up times; and Module 12, Program Management should include a staff planning meeting.

Observing the Staff Member with Children

Your documentation of the observation is an important aspect of the Competency Assessment. It should provide a picture of how the staff member interacts with and responds to children. It is not possible to capture everything that takes place, but it is important to record as much as possible because this data will be used to determine competence. Observation notes should provide an objective description of what happened that you can share with the staff member. To be useful, observation notes should have the following characteristics:

- **Objectivity:** Include only the facts about what happens, not labels, judgments, or inferences. Record only what the staff member does and says and what the children do and say in response.

- **Specificity:** Record as much information as possible to present a picture of the staff member's actions. Include details such as the number of children involved, where indoors or outdoors the action is taking place, words and tone of voice used.

- **Accuracy:** Record the staff member's and children's actions and words directly and in the order in which they happen. Try to include direct quotes whenever possible.

- **Completeness:** Include descriptions of activities from beginning to end. Record information about the setting (the number and ages of children, where indoors or outdoors the action is taking place), what the staff member does, what is said, and the children's verbal and nonverbal responses.

Scoring the Assessments and Discussing the Results

Most adults are eager to know the results of their work. Therefore, it is important to score the assessments and share the results with the staff member as soon as possible. During a meeting with the staff member, you will discuss the answers to the Knowledge Assessment and what you saw and heard during the observation period.

The answer sheets for the Knowledge Assessments are found in Appendix B. Scoring for each question is indicated on the answer sheets. Some questions have more than one possible correct response, also indicated on the answer sheets. A perfect score is 100. To complete the Knowledge Assessment successfully, a staff member must obtain a score of at least 80 percent.

When a staff member does not achieve a passing score on the Knowledge Assessment, review the answers together. Trainers need to judge how much support the staff member needs to understand fully the material presented in the module. As stated earlier, the goal is to ensure competence and understanding, not simply to have the staff member pass the test. You might suggest reviewing specific Learning Activities or provide additional resources. Staff can let you know when they are ready to schedule the retest.

To score the Competency Assessment, use the notes from the observation and others in the past month to rate whether each criterion of competence was met, partially met, or not met. If you did not observe a criterion, you should leave the rating blank. Here is an excerpt from the rating page of the Competency Assesment for Module 10, Guidance.

MODULE 10: GUIDANCE

Prior to the observation period, assess the following criteria.

The Competent Staff Member Will:

Follow a daily schedule that allows children to choose their own activities.
[ ] met   [ ] partially met   [ ] not met

Make sure there are no safety hazards in the environment.
[ ] met   [ ] partially met   [ ] not met

Next, review your ratings and determine whether the staff member has successfully demonstrated competence. When a staff member has clearly demonstrated the skills identified in the criteria for assessment, offer congratulations, along with some examples of competence drawn from the observation notes. If a staff member has demonstrated some of the skills but has not thoroughly applied the knowledge presented in the module, you will need to handle the meeting differently.

The goal of the assessment is to validate competency. Adult learners generally know when they have not demonstrated the needed skills to complete an assessment successfully. It is not helpful to assess a staff member as competent when he or she still needs more support and training. If a skill has not been mastered, use the meeting as an opportunity to reassess training needs and to provide additional support.

Here are some suggestions for discussing the Competency Assessment results.

- **Begin the conference by asking for the staff member's comments.** "How do you feel about what took place?" "Did everything go as you had planned?" "Were there any surprises?"

- **Sort out what went well and what problems existed, if any.** "What do you think went well?" "Is there anything you would want to do differently?"

- **Share your observation notes with the staff member.** "Let's look at my notes on what happened and see what we can learn from them."

- **Review the criteria together.** Ask the staff member to assess which skills were clearly demonstrated and which ones were not.

- **Give the decision and explain the reasoning behind it.**

   - If the staff member has clearly demonstrated competence, appears to understand the information, and can apply it consistently in working with children, offer congratulations and take a few minutes to share observations of the individual's progress.

   - If the staff member has not met the criteria for competence, state your decision and explain why you think he or she needs more time to develop the necessary skills. Discuss the identified weaknesses, giving examples from your observation notes. Then discuss what form of support would be most helpful and develop a plan to work together. Reassure the staff member that he or she can redo the Competency Assessment after spending further time developing skills.

As staff members work on other modules, it is a good idea to periodically review their competence in using the skills developed in previous ones. There may be times when a trainer's observations indicate that a staff member needs to repeat a module or at least some of the Learning Activities as a "skill refresher."

The following section includes copies of the Knowledge Assessments for all 13 modules followed by Competency Assessments for Modules 1 through 12. Appendix B includes answer sheets for the Knowledge Assessments and Appendix C includes trainer observation forms for the Competency Assessments.

Knowledge Assessments

Knowledge Assessment
Module 1: Safe

Multiple Choice. Put an "X" on the line next to the best answer from those given.

1. To keep children safe while outdoors in a lightning storm,

    a. _____ seek shelter in a vehicle or low area.

    b. _____ stay away from isolated trees.

    c. _____ stay away from water.

    d. _____ don't touch or stand near metal objects.

    e. _____ all of the above.

2. A staff member should call for emergency assistance immediately under the following conditions:

    a. _____ a child vomits.

    b. _____ a child is unconscious.

    c. _____ a child loses a baby tooth.

    d. _____ a child's bleeding does not stop when direct pressure is applied to the wound.

    e. _____ b and d.

3. To keep children safe after an earthquake,

    a. _____ light some emergency candles.

    b. _____ turn on the lights to see if anyone is injured.

    c. _____ wait patiently in case there are additional shocks.

    d. _____ turn on a transistor radio and listen for emergency instructions.

    e. _____ c and d.

4. When walking with children in traffic,

    a. _____ always cross at crosswalks and obey traffic signals.

    b. _____ let the older children run ahead and wait for the group at the corner.

    c. _____ assign one adult to be with children who tend to act before thinking.

    d. _____ a and c.

    e. _____ none of the above.

5. To prevent accidents,

    a. _____ change an activity when children become tired or over-heated.

    b. _____ work with colleagues to supervise all indoor and outdoor areas.

    c. _____ participate in active games and sports with children.

    d. _____ monitor children's arrivals and departures.

    e. _____ all of the above.

Short Answers. Complete the following exercises. Some require more than one response. Partial credit will be given.

6. List **two** safety rules to follow when setting up a school-age program environment.

    a. _____

    b. _____

7. List **two** examples of items to check daily to maintain safety indoors.

    a. _____

    b. _____

8. List **two** examples of items to check monthly to maintain safety outdoors.

    a. _____

    b. _____

9. Think of an emergency situation that might arise at the program and list **two** things staff could do to keep children safe in that situation.

    Emergency situation: _____

    a. _____

    b. _____

10. Explain why it is important to involve children in setting safety rules?

    _____

    _____

    _____

11. Emily gets separated from the group while on a field trip to the zoo. List the rules and procedures Emily should follow. (Children and staff reviewed these before the trip.)

    _____

    _____

    _____

12. List **two** steps to take before a field trip.

    a. _____

    b. _____

13. Describe **two** ways staff can help children learn to keep themselves safe.

    a. _____

    b. _____

14. Explain what the Code of Ethical Conduct of the National Association of the Education of Young Children (Principle 1.1) means to you:

    Above all we shall not harm children. We shall not participate in practices
    that are disrespectful, degrading, dangerous, exploitive, intimidating,
    psychologically damaging, or physically harmful to children.

    _____

    _____

    _____

    _____

    _____

    _____

    _____

Knowledge Assessment
Module 2: Healthy

Multiple Choice. Put an "X" on the line next to the best answer from those given.

1. People who are healthy

    a. _____ are well rested, energetic, and strong.

    b. _____ exercise regularly.

    c. _____ feel good about themselves.

    d. _____ get along well with others.

    e. _____ all of the above.

2. Staff and children should wash their hands

    a. _____ before and after preparing or eating food.

    b. _____ after using the bathroom.

    c. _____ when arriving at the program.

    d. _____ after outdoor activities.

    e. _____ all of the above.

3. Staff can help children develop healthy habits by

    a. _____ offering a variety of healthy foods for snacks.

    b. _____ inviting a nutritionist to give a presentation at the program.

    c. _____ helping children set up and care for a vegetable garden.

    d. _____ providing a self-service snack area.

    e. _____ all of the above.

4. HIV (Human Immunodeficiency Virus) can be transmitted by

    a. _____ sexual intercourse with someone infected with HIV.

    b. _____ sharing the bathroom with someone with HIV.

    c. _____ hugging and kissing an HIV-infected person.

    d. _____ being in the same room with an HIV-infected person.

    e. _____ a and d.

Short Answers. Complete the following exercises. Some require more than one response. Partial credit will be given.

5. Name **two** things to do to maintain a hygienic indoor and outdoor environment.

    a. _____

    b. _____

6. Name **two** things to look for when conducting a daily child health check.

    a. _____

    b. _____

7. For **two** common childhood illnesses, describe the symptoms and explain when the child is no longer contagious.

    a. _____

    _____

    b. _____

    _____

8. List **two** potential sources of short-term stress for children.

    a. _____

    b. _____

9. List **two** ways the school-age program can reduce sources of stress.

    a. _____

    b. _____

10. Describe a stressful situation either you or a child in your program experienced and the strategies you used to handle the situation.

    _____

    _____

    _____

    _____

11. Describe what you must do if you suspect a child in the program is being abused or neglected.

    _____

    _____

    _____

    _____

Matching.

12. Match each type of child abuse named in the left column with the appropriate definition in the right column. Write the correct number on the line.

Type of Abuse	Definition
a. _____ Neglect	1. Using a child in any sexual context, including fondling, rape, sodomy, and using a child in pornographic pictures or film.
b. _____ Emotional abuse/maltreatment	2. Failure to provide a child with food, clothing, medical attention, or supervision.
c. _____ Physical abuse	3 Behavior on part of offender which includes blaming, belittling, ridiculing, badgering, and constantly ignoring a child's needs.
d. _____ Sexual abuse	4. Action including burning, kicking, biting, punching, slapping, or hitting a child.

Knowledge Assessment
Module 3: Program Environment

Multiple Choice. Put an "X" on the line next to the best answer from those given.

1. An appropriate program environment:

    a. _____ has soft, cozy areas where children can play alone or with others.

    b. _____ provides sufficient space for children's personal belongings.

    c. _____ complements rather than duplicates the school day.

    d. _____ provides opportunities for many kinds of activities.

    e. _____ all of the above.

2. Interest areas in shared space should be

    a. _____ avoided, because there isn't time to set them up each day.

    b. _____ offered from time to time.

    c. _____ created as portable modules or kits.

    d. _____ created once, at the beginning of the year.

    e. _____ c and d.

3. A good schedule for a school-age program provides

    a. _____ sufficient time for transitions and cleanup.

    b. _____ very little free choice time, so children don't get into trouble.

    c. _____ large blocks of time when all the children participate in the same activity.

    d. _____ the same activities every day.

    e. _____ b and c.

Short Answers. Complete the following exercises. Some require more than one response. Partial credit will be given.

4. Describe **one** indoor interest area and the kinds of activities children might do there.

    Interest area: _____

    _____

    Activities: _____

    _____

    _____

5. When selecting materials for the school-age program, **two** questions to ask are:

    a. _____

    b. _____

6. List **two** items that might be found in each of the following interest areas.

    a. Quiet area: _____

    b. Dramatic play area: _____

    c. Math area: _____

    d. Blocks and construction area: _____

    e. Arts and crafts area: _____

7. For one interest area, describe **two** sub-areas that might be created to respond to children's interests.

    Area: _____

    a. _____

    b. _____

8. Describe **two** ways to use the outdoor environment creatively.

    a. _____

    b. _____

9. Describe a transition time in your program and what you do to make it go smoothly.

    _____

    _____

    _____

    _____

10. Choose one age group (5- to 7-years, 8- to 10-years, or 11- to 12-years) and describe **five** ways children in that age group typically use the environment.

    Age group: _____

    a. _____

    b. _____

    c. _____

    d. _____

    e. _____

11. Name **two** materials that can be used for the following outdoor activities:

    a. Water play:_____

    b. Hot-weather play: _____

    c. Sand play: _____

    d. Physical play: _____

    e. Construction: _____

12. List **two** criteria for an appropriate after-school schedule for a school-age program.

    a. _____

    b. _____

Knowledge Assessment
Module 4: Physical

Short Answers. Complete the following exercises. Some require more than one response. Partial credit will be given.

1. Describe **two** characteristics of the physical development of 5- to 7-year-old children.

   a. _____

   b. _____

2. Describe **two** characteristics of the physical development of 8- to 10-year-old children.

   a. _____

   b. _____

3. Describe **two** characteristics of the physical development of 11- to 12-year-old children.

   a. _____

   b. _____

4. The **three** categories of basic gross motor skills are identified below. For each one, give an example of how children (and adults) use the skill in routines, sports, and games.

   a. Object control: _____

   b. Locomotor: _____

   c. Non locomotor: _____

5. How can movement stations support children's physical development?

   _____

   _____

6. Larry (8 years) is new to playing softball. He doesn't want to try to swing at the ball. What could a staff member do and say privately to encourage Larry?

   _____

   _____

7. The **four** essential elements of cooperative games are identified below. Think of a cooperative game and describe how it includes these elements.

   Game: _____

   a. Cooperation: _____

   b. Acceptance: _____

   c. Involvement: _____

   d. Fun: _____

8. Describe an activity that encourages children to use their senses (sight, sound, touch, taste, and smell) as they coordinate fine motor skills.

_____

_____

_____

_____

_____

_____

9. Select **one** competitive sport or game and describe how to make it a cooperative one.

Sport or game: _____

_____

_____

10. Pick **one** interest area and describe how a child might use fine motor skills in that area.

Interest area: _____

_____

_____

_____

Matching.

11. Match each activity on the left with the appropriate objective on the right. Write the number on the line.

Physical Fitness Activity	Objectives
a. ____ Fitness Club	1. Practice skills to improve performance in game or sport.
b. ____ Obstacle course	2. Use equipment such as jump ropes and balls in a place designed especially for such use.
c. ____ World dance prop box	3. Participate with others who share an interest in a physical activity.
d. ____ Sports clinic	4. Learn about traditional dances from other countries.
e. ____ Exercise activity center	5. Maneuver a course that has challenging objects to overcome.

Knowledge Assessment
Module 5: Cognitive

Matching.

1. Match the characteristics of children's cognitive development with the appropriate age group. Write the letter on the line.

Age Groups
a. 5- to 7-years   b. 8- to 10-years   c. 11- to 12-years

1. _____ They like to collect and catalogue things.

2. _____ They are eager to learn the answers to "why" questions.

3. _____ They understand explanations and rules and enjoy following rules to the letter.

4. _____ They show proficiency in particular skills and talents.

5. _____ They still need to work with real objects to grasp number concepts.

6. _____ They appreciate other people's points of view.

7. _____ They are beginning to understand time, but may not understand past and future.

8. _____ They think in abstract terms.

9. _____ They may be critical of their own performance.

Multiple Choice. Put an "X" on the line next to the best answer from those given.

2. Cognitive development is

   a. _____ the collective sum of information a child has.

   b. _____ the process of learning to think and reason.

   c. _____ the result of worksheets, assignments, drill, and practice.

   d. _____ a set of skills promoted only through formal education.

   e. _____ all of the above.

3. One of the best ways to encourage children's problem-solving is to:

   a. _____ give them homework on problem-solving.

   b. _____ reward them for correct responses.

   c. _____ show your own interest in learning about the world.

   d. _____ punish them for incorrect responses.

   e. _____ none of the above.

Short Answers. Complete the following exercises. Some require more than one response. Partial credit will be given.

4. a. Why is it important for children to learn how to learn? _____

    _____

    b. What can you to do help children become good learners? _____

    _____

5. Choose one interest area and describe **two** materials to include there so children can use their cognitive skills.

    Interest area: _____

    a. _____

    b. _____

6. List **two** ways to offer support at each of the following stages in the learning cycle while a child learns to roller skate. (You can use another example if you prefer.)

    Awareness:

    a. _____

    b. _____

    Exploration:

    a. _____

    b. _____

    Inquiry:

    a. _____

    b. _____

    Utilization:

    a. _____

    b. _____

7. Several children are interested in how much light plants need to grow. They want to conduct an experiment. Using the **five** steps in the scientific method, explain how they could set up their experiment. (You can use another example if you prefer.)

    a. Gather information: _____

    _____

    b. State the problem clearly: _____

    _____

    c. Generate ideas: _____

    _____

d. Evaluate the answers and select a "best" option: _____

_____

e. Test out the option: _____

_____

8. How do the following questions encourage children to think before answering and stimulate further thinking?

a. What do you think the boy in the story should do? _____

_____

b. What can you tell me about dinosaurs? _____

_____

c. Why do you think the plants in our garden are doing so well? _____

_____

d. Can you think of some ways to make our field trip really special? _____

_____

Matching.

9. Match each area of intelligence named in the left column with the appropriate skill identified in the right column. Write the number on the line.

Gardner's Areas of Intelligence	Skills
a. _____ Logical	1. Relates well to others, shows younger children how to do things.
b. _____ Linguistic	2. Recognizes instruments by hearing a piece of music, sings in harmony.
c. _____ Musical	3. Solves difficult puzzles, calculates math problems with ease.
d. _____ Spatial	4. Performs well in gym or dance, takes apart and rebuilds a radio or clock.
e. _____ Bodily kinesthetic	5. Sets and pursues long-term goals, advises a friend on a personal problem.
f. _____ Interpersonal	6. Writes poems and plays, reads a wide variety of books.
g. _____ Intrapersonal	7. Designs and builds an obstacle course.

10. Match each thinking skill in the left column with the appropriate example in the right column. Write the number on the line.

Thinking Skill	Example of Use
a. _____ Noticing characteristics of things	1. Lily sorted her stamp collection by country.
b. _____ Classifying	2. Jack put the board games on the shelf by size, with the largest ones on the bottom.
c. _____ Sequencing	3. Peter smelled the spices before deciding which ones to put in the muffins.
d. _____ Understanding cause and effect	4. Wanda moved the paint to the middle of the table so it wouldn't be knocked over by someone walking by.

Knowledge Assessment
Module 6: Communication

Matching.

1. Match the characteristics of children's development with the appropriate age group. Write the letter on the line.

> **Age Groups**
>
> **a. 5- to 7-years   b. 8- to 10-years   c. 11- to 12-years**

1. _____ They like to socialize with friends.

2. _____ They ask seemingly endless questions.

3. _____ They use a lot of slang and "fad" words.

4. _____ They often exaggerate, boast, and tell tall tales.

5. _____ They may question rules and beliefs they previously accepted.

6. _____ They often can speak with the fluency of adults.

7. _____ They like coded languages and passwords.

8. _____ They can be intolerant of different accents or languages.

9. _____ They are interested in the meaning of words.

Multiple Choice. Put an "X" on the line next to the best answer from those given.

2. Learning to use language as a way to communicate with others is important because

    a. _____ social development is dependent on language.

    b. _____ the ability to put feelings and thoughts into words affects self-esteem.

    c. _____ language is a way to express our thoughts and feelings.

    d. _____ language development is related to cognitive development.

    e. _____ all of the above.

3. School-age staff can support children's reading skills by

    a. _____ insisting that children look up any words they don't know.

    b. _____ providing a wide range of interesting books and magazines.

    c. _____ letting children read to them.

    d. _____ serving as a positive role model.

    e. _____ b, c, and d.

Short Answers. Complete the following exercises. Some require more than one response. Partial credit will be given.

4. Give **two** reasons why children and staff should use "I" messages.

   a. _____

   _____

   b. _____

   _____

5. Give **three** examples of ways a school-age program can provide meaningful opportunities for children to write.

   a. _____

   _____

   b. _____

   _____

   c. _____

   _____

6. Choose one interest area and describe **two** materials to include there so children can use their communication skills.

   Interest area: _____

   a. _____

   b. _____

7. List **three** magazines to which your program subscribes and explain how each one matches the communication skills and interests of the children enrolled.

   a. _____

   _____

   b. _____

   _____

   c. _____

   _____

8. Describe **two** ways children benefit from putting their feelings into words.

   a. _____

   b. _____

9. For each of the following communication skills, give **two** examples of how children might use the skill: one at the program and one at home.

Communication Skill	Use at the Program	Use at Home
Listening		
Speaking		
Reading		
Writing		

Knowledge Assessment
Module 7: Creative

Multiple Choice. Put an "X" on the line next to the best answer from those given.

1. Which of the following activities probably could be considered "creative?"

    a. _____ baking bread by following a cookbook recipe exactly.

    b. _____ filling in a coloring book.

    c. _____ developing a new fruit by using knowledge of botany.

    d. _____ taking several photographs of the same object by experimenting with angles.

    e. _____ c and d.

2. How can school-age staff promote children's creativity?

    a. _____ by requiring children to participate in craft activities.

    b. _____ by allowing them to make messes and mistakes.

    c. _____ by providing models of good art for them to copy.

    d. _____ by reminding children that their skills are limited.

    e. _____ all of the above.

3. Which is important when planning and conducting activities that encourage creativity?

    a. _____ giving very detailed instructions.

    b. _____ making a model, so everyone knows what to do.

    c. _____ trying the activity yourself before introducing it to the children.

    d. _____ never commenting on children's work so they won't be self-conscious.

    e. _____ a and b.

Short Answers. Complete the following exercises. Some require more than one response. Partial credit will be given.

4. Ms. Jensen planned a creative writing activity using her collection of stamps from around the world. Each child selected a stamp and wrote an imaginary letter to a child from the country the stamp came from. The children were fascinated by the stamps. They said they wanted to design their own. What could Ms. Jensen do to extend their interest?

    _____

    _____

    _____

5. List **two** characteristics of a school-age program that motivate children to be creative.

    a. _____

    b. _____

6. Describe how children used their creativity during a long-term project that took place at the school-age program.

    _____

    _____

    _____

    _____

    _____

    _____

    _____

7. List **two** open-ended materials provided at the school-age program and describe how children use them.

    a. Material: _____

    How children use it: _____

    _____

    b. Material: _____

    How children use it: _____

    _____

8. Describe something you did recently that used creativity.

    _____

    _____

    _____

    _____

9. Yancey (9 years) is motivated to learn about training animals because he finds it interesting and satisfying. List **four** ways staff can support him as he explores his interests?

    a. _____

    _____

    b. _____

    _____

    c. _____

    _____

    d. _____

    _____

True or False?

10. For each statement that is true, write T on the line. For each statement that is false, write F.

a. _____ Highly creative children are always extremely intelligent.

b. _____ A typical 5-year-old is likely to be more interested in hammering nails than making a birdfeeder.

c. _____ A typical 9-year-old does not worry about whether her drawing is "good."

d. _____ Children can use all of their skills in creative pursuits.

e. _____ It is important to have lots of competitions at the program so children will know if their work is any good.

f. _____ A typical 11-year-old wants to be different from his friends.

g. _____ Often creativity involves being messy and making mistakes.

h. _____ Staff should not model their own creativity because the children will be intimidated.

Matching.

11. Match each step in the creative process, identified in the column on the left, with the appropriate example from the column on the right. Write the number on the line.

Steps in the Creative Process	Example
a. ____ Preparation	1. Rashid shares his idea with Mr. Thorne and announces his project at group meeting. He asks other children to work with him.
b. ____ Incubation	2. Rashid makes a list of all the ideas he is considering. He puts them in categories: easy to do, hard to do, and impossible. He goes outside with the Jogging Club.
c. ____ Illumination	3. Rashid thinks about potential projects as he runs. He comes inside and works on an idea—raising flower and vegetable seedlings to donate to a senior citizens home.
d. ____ Verification/communication	4. Rashid wants to start a unique community service project—something no one has done before. He looks in *The Kids Can Help Book* for ideas.

Knowledge Assessment
Module 8: Self

Short Answers. Complete the following exercises. Some require more than one response. Partial credit will be given.

1. Name **three** things staff can do to foster children's self-esteem.

   a. _____

   b. _____

   c. _____

2. Think of a child in the program who has high self-esteem. With this child in mind, complete the following statement.   This child

   feels **connected** to: _____

   _____

   has a sense of being **unique** because: _____

   _____

   feels **powerful** enough to: _____

   _____

   has adult models for behavior, including: _____

   _____

3. Give **two** examples of how the school-age program gives children opportunities to "feel successful and competent."

   a. _____

   b. _____

4. Rewrite each statement so it will convey respect.

   a. "Todd, you're always dropping things, are your fingers broken?"

   _____

   _____

   b. "Kwami, didn't I tell you that fighting is wrong? Can't you remember anything?"

   _____

   _____

   c. "You should behave more like your older sister Yvonne."

   _____

   _____

5. What are **two** ways to help children accept and appreciate themselves and others?

   a. _____

   b. _____

6. Describe something about yourself or something you do that you are proud of.

   _____

   _____

7. Identify one of the easiest ways to learn about children: _____

Multiple Choice. Put an "X" on the line next to the best answer from those given.

8. To respond to each child as an individual, it is important to

   a. _____ get to know each child and the context in which he or she is growing up.

   b. _____ be aware of the developmental stages and characteristics of school-age children.

   c. _____ listen to and respond to children.

   d. _____ be aware of one's biases and learn to be open to different ways of thinking.

   e. _____ all of the above.

True or False?

9. For each statement that is true, write T on the line. For each statement that is false, write F.

   a. _____ Talking respectfully with children is an important way to foster their self-esteem.

   b. _____ Providing the right level of support requires knowledge of individual children's capabilities and temperament.

   c. _____ Your own experiences should never affect your relationships with the children in the program.

   d. _____ Children learn to think and solve problems when they can voice their ideas and opinions.

   e. _____ Attention Deficit Disorder and learning disabilities affect children at school, but not at a school-age program

   f. _____ Children should participate in group activities at the program and pursue individual interests at home.

   g. _____ Children want to be liked and accepted by their peers.

   h. _____ When children make mistakes while using the program's supplies staff should stop them immediately so they don't waste materials.

i. _____ Allowing children to take leadership roles helps them develop self-confidence.

j. _____ Sometimes you may need to take your anger out on children in order to maintain control.

Matching.

10. Match each developmental stage in the column on the left with its respective age characteristic in the column on the right. Write the number on the line.

Erikson's Developmental Stage	Characteristics
a. ____ Autonomy	1. Preschoolers are active, talkative, and creative.
b. ____ Industry	2. Infants feel safe, cared for, and valued.
c. ____ Initiative	3. School-age children feel proud as they master skills and develop a realistic self-image.
d. ____ Industry	4. Toddlers are independent and learn to do things for themselves.

11. Describe how your own sense of self and self-esteem affect your relationships with children in the program.

_____

_____

_____

_____

_____

_____

Knowledge Assessment
Module 9: Social

Matching.

1. Match characteristics of children's social development with the appropriate age group. Write the letter on the line.

> **Age Group**
>
> **a. 5- to 7-years   b. 8- to 10-years   c. 11- to 12-years**

1. ____   They can be very competitive and may get upset if they lose a game.

2. ____   They are defining what it means to be a boy or girl.

3. ____   They learn to accept responsibility for their actions.

4. ____   They question rules and beliefs that used to be accepted without thinking.

5. ____   They experience feelings such as sadness and joy deeply, as adults do.

6. ____   They learn best through play.

7. ____   They tend to be unaware of other people's points of view.

8. ____   Their self-esteem is related to how others see them.

9. ____   They may be in a hurry to grow up.

Short Answers. Complete the following exercises. Some require more than one response. Partial credit will be given.

2. Greenspan describes five milestones of emotional development: security, relating, intentional two-way communication without words, emotional ties, and emotional thinking. Select **three** milestones and describe what children who have accomplished the milestone can do.

a. Milestone: _____

_____

_____

b. Milestone:_____

_____

_____

c. Milestone:_____

_____

_____

3. Sara Smilansky has identified four kinds of play enjoyed by school-age children. For each one, give an example that describes children engaged in this type of play.

   a. Functional play:_____

   _____

   b. Constructive play:_____

   _____

   c. Games with rules:_____

   _____

   d. Socio-dramatic play:_____

   _____

4. The following **five** techniques can be used to help children master emotional milestones. For each one give an example of how staff could use it.

   a. One-on-one time: _____

   _____

   b. Problem-solving time: _____

   _____

   c. Identifying and empathizing with a child's point of view: _____

   _____

   d. Breaking the challenge into small pieces: _____

   _____

   e. Setting limits: _____

   _____

5. Describe **two** ways to help a shy or withdrawn child learn to make friends.

   a. _____

   b. _____

6. Give **two** examples of strategies your school-age program uses to encourages children to become involved in the larger community.

   a. _____

   _____

   b. _____

   _____

7. Ms. Yannick sees Davida trying to join in a jump rope game with Lisa, Neville, and Tatia. Davida jumps in with Lisa. The other girls stop and tell her: "Who asked you to join? Get out of the way." Davida snatches the rope and refuses to give it back. How could Ms. Yannick intervene to help Davida learn how to join in a game or activity with other children?

_____

_____

_____

_____

_____

8. Describe your program's ground rules for group meetings.

_____

_____

_____

_____

_____

_____

True or False?

9. For each statement that is true, write T on the line. For each statement that is false, write F.

a. _____ By the time children enter school they have already acquired a wide range of social skills.

b. _____ School-age children aren't emotionally ready to learn how to negotiate and resolve conflicts.

c. _____ It is not a good idea to offer multi-age activities because the older and younger children tend to fight with each other.

d. _____ Group meetings can foster a sense of community among the children in the program.

Knowledge Assessment
Module 10: Guidance

Multiple Choice. Put an "X" on the line next to the best answer from those given.

1. Which of the following elements of the physical environment support children's self-discipline?

    a. _____ The daily schedule is posted where children can see it.

    b. _____ The program's sponges, mops, and brooms are stored in a locked closet.

    c. _____ Children share the storage areas for personal belongings—first come, first served is the program practice.

    d. _____ Active games must take place outdoors.

    e. _____ None of the above.

2. Which of the following program practices help to reduce conflicts?

    a. _____ Staff make all the rules and review them with children every day before activities can begin.

    b. _____ There are weekly contests and athletic tournaments.

    c. _____ Each person's unique characteristics are appreciated and valued.

    d. _____ Children and staff have good communication skills.

    e. _____ c and d.

3. What should staff do when children have negative feelings?

    a. _____ Recognize and accept their feelings.

    b. _____ Help children to express their feelings in acceptable ways.

    c. _____ Tell children, "You have nothing to feel bad about. Get out of that bad mood."

    d. _____ Make children join in a group activity so they will forget about their problems.

    e. _____ a and b.

4. Why are children under age 9 likely to follow rules?

    a. _____ They believe in human rights.

    b. _____ They don't want to be punished.

    c. _____ They feel good when they do the "right thing."

    d. _____ They know it is their duty.

    e. _____ b and c.

Short Answers. Complete the following exercises. Some require more than one response. Partial credit will be given.

5. "SIGEP" is the acronym for a **five**-step conflict resolution technique. Identify a typical conflict that might arise at the school-age program. Describe how children could use the SIGEP strategy to solve it.

   Problem or conflict: _____

   _____

   a. Stop: _____

   _____

   b. Identify: _____

   _____

   c. Generate: _____

   _____

   d. Evaluate: _____

6. State **two** positive guidance techniques staff can use to help children learn self-discipline.

   a. _____

   b. _____

7. What is the difference between punishment and discipline?

   _____

   _____

   _____

8. Describe the procedure used to mediate a conflict.

   _____

   _____

   _____

9. For each example in column one, describe the possible cause and how staff could respond to guide children's behavior.

Children's Behavior	Possible Cause	How Staff Could Respond
a. Tara and Carlos (12 years) constantly complain about being too old for the program.		
b. Josie and Kahil (6 years) resist clean-up. They won't put things away at the end of the day.		
c. Ruth (8 years) doesn't play with the other children. She just sits and reads.		
d. Victor (9 years) wanders from one activity to the next, never finishing or getting involved.		

Matching.

10. Match each conflict resolution technique in the left column with its appropriate description in the right column. Write the number on the line.

Conflict Resolution Technique	Description
a. ____ Storytelling	1. Children reflect on the problem for a few minutes and try to solve it.
b. ____ Planning Time	2. Children reenact the problem for an audience, stopping at the point of conflict. The group discusses possible solutions.
c. ____ Role Playing	3. A staff member listens as children describe the conflict, then restates the children's words.
d. ____ Role Reversal	4. Children begin to reenact the problem, then switch roles to see the situation from a different perspective. The group then discusses possible solutions.
e. ____ Reflective Listening	5. A staff member retells what occurred in the form of a story.

True or False?

11. For each statement that is true, write T on the line. For each statement that is false, write F.

a. _____ Rules and limits help children and adults understand what behaviors are acceptable.

b. _____ It is more effective to tell people what they should not do than what they should do.

c. _____ Children behave appropriately when the rules and limits never change.

d. _____ Children are more likely to follow rules better if they understand the reasons behind them.

e. _____ Children are more likely to follow rules if they help create them.

Knowledge Assessment
Module 11: Families

Short Answers. Complete the following exercises. Some require more than one response. Partial credit will be given.

1. Describe **two** to encourage parents to participate in their child's life at the program.

    a. _____

    _____

    b. _____

    _____

2. List **four** things that parents are more likely to know and **four** things that staff might know about a child.

Parents	Staff
a. _____	_____
b. _____	_____
c. _____	_____
d. _____	_____

3. Give an example of **one** technique the school-age program uses to keep parents informed about activities.

    _____

    _____

    _____

4. Describe how to prepare for and conduct a parent-staff conference.

    Prepare for: _____

    _____

    _____

    _____

    Conduct: _____

    _____

    _____

    _____

5. Give **two** examples of events that can be sources of stress for parents.

   a. _____

   b. _____

6. Name **two** things staff can do to help parents locate community resources.

   a. _____

   b. _____

7. Describe **two** ways to maintain a strong partnership with parents.

   a. _____

   b. _____

8. List **five** topics to include in a parent handbook.

   a. _____

   b. _____

   c. _____

   d. _____

   e. _____

9. Describe what you find most rewarding about working with parents.

   _____

   _____

   _____

True or False?

10. For each statement that is true, write <u>T</u> on the line. For each statement that is false, write <u>F</u>.

   a. _____ Parents are the most important people in children's lives.

   b. _____ It is best to wait until parents ask for information about their child's activities at the program.

   c. _____ Most parents are concerned about what is best for thir children.

   d. _____ Parents should <u>always</u> let staff know when they are going to visit the program because children are upset by unannounced visits.

   e. _____ Staff should not bother parents by asking them about their children's interests.

Knowledge Assessment
Module 12: Program Management

Multiple Choice. Put an "X" on the line next to the best answer from those given.

1. Clubs allow school-age children to

   a. _____ do their homework.

   b. _____ explore topics of special interest.

   c. _____ stay busy so staff can do their paperwork.

   d. _____ carry out their own plans.

   e. _____ b and d.

2. An example from an objective observation recording is,

   a. _____ Derrick was too lazy to pick up the bat.

   b. _____ Derrick, a mature 9-year-old.

   c. _____ Derrick walked past the bat.

   d. _____ Derrick did not like the game.

   e. _____ Derrick was not a good hitter.

Short Answers. Complete the following exercises. Some require more than one response. Partial credit will be given.

3. List **five** steps staff should take when planning how to include a child with a diagnosed disability in the program.

   a. _____

   b. _____

   c. _____

   d. _____

   e. _____

4. Give **two** reasons why staff observe children.

   a. _____

   b. _____

5. Describe an action you took recently to individualize the program for one or more children.

   _____

   _____

   _____

6. Write an open-ended question that could be included in a survey to solicit parent's ideas for new program activities.

_____

_____

7. It is helpful to use planning categories when developing weekly plans. Name **two** categories that might be useful for your program.

a. _____

b. _____

8. Give an example that shows how to use an open-ended material or activity to individualize the program.

_____

_____

_____

9. List **two** administrative policies and procedures you follow every day.

a. _____

b. _____

10. Describe **two** ways you involve children as members of the team that plans the program.

a. _____

b. _____

11. Describe **two** techniques staff can use to observe children systematically.

a. _____

b. _____

True or False?

12. For each statement that is true, write T on the line. For each statement that is false, write F.

a. _____ It is best for one person to conduct all observations of a child.

b. _____ Children are constantly growing and changing.

c. _____ It is important to ask children about their needs and interests.

d. _____ Special interest clubs are not appropriate for school-age children.

e. _____ It is appropriate for staff to provide input on program policies.

Knowledge Assessment
Module 13: Professionalism

Short Answers. Complete the following exercises. Some require more than one response. Partial credit will be given.

1. Write a brief description of yourself. What strengths and abilities do you apply in your work? What do you enjoy most about being a school-age professional?

   _____

   _____

   _____

   _____

   _____

   _____

   _____

   _____

   _____

2. Why is it important to continually expand your knowledge and professional skills?

   _____

   _____

   _____

3. Name **two** ways a professional can continue learning.

   a. _____

   b. _____

4. Give an example of an ethic that applies to school-age professionals and the professional behavior that goes with it.

   Ethic: _____

   _____

   Behavior: _____

   _____

5. What is an advocate for children and families?

   _____

   _____

6. Name **two** ways to become an advocate for children and families.

   a. _____

   b. _____

7. Name **two** ways you can take care of yourself.

Physically:

a. _____

b. _____

Emotionally:

a. _____

b. _____

Socially:

a. _____

b. _____

Intellectually:

a. _____

b. _____

8. List **two** topics related to working with school-age children you want to learn more about.

a. _____

b. _____

9. Mr. Cannon, a school-age staff member, is walking back inside the building He sees Ms. Diamond, another staff member, watching the children's softball game while smoking a cigarette—which is a violation of the program's policies. What should he do?

_____

_____

_____

_____

True or False?

10. For each statement that is true, write T on the line. For each statement that is false, write F.

a. _____ A professional is someone with specialized knowledge and skills.

b. _____ Working with school-age children is not a real profession.

c. _____ It is unprofessional to speak out against inappropriate school practices.

d. _____ School-age professionals show no bias against any children in the program.

e. _____ Confidentiality related to families is only important within the program.

Competency Assessments

Competency Assessment
Module 1: Safe

Before the observation period your trainer will assess whether you use skills such as the following:

- Conducting safety checks (daily and monthly, indoor and outdoor); removing or repairing unsafe items; keeping safety equipment in good condition; and maintaining first-aid and safety supplies.

- Checking daily to see that equipment and supplies are cleaned up and stored appropriately.

- Arranging the program space so there are clear traffic paths and exits.

- Designating separate areas for quiet and active play to avoid congestion and collisions.

- Arranging the environment so that children and staff are visible at all times.

- Making sure there is an accessible telephone in working order.

- Limiting access to supplies and equipment for children who do not yet have the skills and judgment to use them safely.

- Developing and posting accident and emergency procedures.

- Stating the correct procedures to follow when there is an accident or emergency.

- Maintaining up-to-date emergency telephone numbers for all parents.

- Monitoring children's arrivals and departures.

- Inviting community representatives to talk with children about safety.

Your trainer will review records from this observation (including an emergency drill) and others conducted in the last month to assess whether you use skills such as the following:

- Protecting and reassuring children while conducting an emergency drill according to established procedures. (You will conduct an emergency drill as part of this Competency Assessment.)

- Responding quickly and calmly to children in distress.

- Intervening immediately when children are involved in unsafe play.

- Maintaining appropriate child-adult ratios and group sizes.

- Planning a daily schedule to include active and quiet play.

- Involving children in making the program's safety rules.

- Explaining rules and procedures for sports and games before play begins.

- Teaching children proper procedures for using, cleaning up, and storing equipment and supplies.

- Modeling ways to take risks.

- Talking calmly with children about potential hazards in the environment.

- Teaching children to observe safety rules when away from the program.

- Reminding children of safety rules and encouraging them to remind each other.

- Changing activities when children are too excited, angry, or tired to play safely.

Competency Assessment
Module 2: Healthy

Before the observation period your trainer will assess whether you use skills such as the following:

- Checking the facility daily for adequate ventilation and lighting, comfortable room temperature, and good sanitation.

- Placing tissues, paper towels, and soap within children's reach.

- Providing resources on health and hygiene.

- Keeping a supply of sanitary pads and tampons in the girls' bathroom and making sure girls know where these items are.

- Stating the program regulations and state laws related to reporting child abuse and neglect, and describing the signs of possible child maltreatment.

- Stating the symptoms of common childhood illnesses, syndromes, and progressive diseases.

Your trainer will review records from this observation and others conducted in the last month to assess whether you use skills such as the following:

- Opening windows daily to let in fresh air (if needed during observation period).

- Cleaning and disinfecting surfaces before using for food preparation.

- Washing hands and encouraging children to wash theirs using techniques recommended by the Centers for Disease Control.

- Completing daily health checks and observing children for signs of illness.

- Providing opportunities for children to plan, prepare, and serve meals and snacks.

- Offering self-service snack so children can determine when, what, and how much to eat.

- Serving "family-style" meals and eating with children in a relaxing manner.

- Encouraging children to drink water and take breaks when exercising or outdoors on hot days.

- Modeling habits that promote good health and nutrition.

- Maintaining a positive, relaxed, and pleasant program atmosphere to reduce tension and stress.

- Helping children learn ways to recognize, reduce, and cope with stress.

- Using a flexible schedule so children can go outdoors, rest, relax, be active, and eat as needed.

- Being alert to changes in children's behavior that may signal abuse or neglect.

- Supporting families and helping them get the services they need.

Competency Assessment
Module 3: Program Environment

Before the observation period your trainer will assess whether you use skills such as the following:

- Creating a variety of well-equipped indoor and outdoor interest areas that reflect children's skills and interests.

- Rotating interest areas or creating sub-areas in response to changing skills and interests.

- Providing sufficient space and appropriate equipment for group games and sports, indoors and outdoors.

- Locating interest areas near resources (such as light and water) used in the area.

- Defining separate spaces, indoors and outdoors, for active and quite play.

- Storing materials on low, open shelves and storage units so they can be easily selected and replaced.

- Providing materials that reflect diversity and show no bias.

- Providing sufficient space for children to safely store their belongings, long-term projects, and works in progress.

- Creating soft, cozy areas where children can play alone, read, listen to music, daydream, or talk with a friend.

- Adapting the environment, if necessary, to make it appropriate for children with special needs.

- Arranging the outdoor area to support a variety of activities

- Helping older children create spaces designated for their use only.

Your trainer will review records from this observation and others conducted in the last month to assess whether you use skills such as the following:

- Involving children when arranging and rearranging the space used by the program.

- Offering a variety of open-ended materials and equipment children can use in different ways.

- Offering a variety of materials and equipment to meet a wide range of skills.

- Observing, talking with, listening to, and surveying children to determine their interests.

- Providing materials that build on interests children develop outside the program.

- Following a schedule that includes long blocks of time when children can choose what they want to do.

- Providing sufficient time in the schedule for children to carry out their plans and do long-term projects.

- Offering a balance of activity choices (active and quiet; indoor and outdoor; individual, small group, and large group).

- Scheduling time for children to nap or rest after morning kindergarten.

- Including sufficient time for clean-up at the end of morning, afternoon, and full-day sessions.

- Allowing children to meet their personal needs on individual schedules.

- Managing transitions so children do not have to wait with nothing to do.

Competency Assessment
Module 4: Physical

Your trainer will review records from this observation and others conducted in the last month to assess whether you use skills such as the following:

- Providing space and time for children to engage in active play every day.

- Encouraging children when they are learning new skills and providing assistance upon request.

- Suggesting ways children can coordinate movement of their large and small muscles.

- Helping children develop an awareness of rhythm so they can coordinate their movements.

- Observing and recording information about each child's physical strengths, interests, and needs.

- Providing a variety of materials and activities to challenge a wide range of physical capabilities.

- Introducing children to games and activities that encourage physical development and cooperation.

- Encouraging children to make up and organize their own games.

- Encouraging children to use their large muscles in daily routines.

- Planning and implementing increasingly difficult activities in which large muscles are used and that promote development of physical skills used in sports and games.

- Providing activities, materials, and equipment that allow all children to develop and maintain physical fitness.

- Making sure that children take breaks from vigorous activity and drink plenty of water to prevent dehydration.

- Introducing new games and activities regularly so children learn different ways to use their muscles.

- Encouraging children to keep track of their own progress, rather than comparing themselves to others.

- Providing activities, materials, and equipment that accommodate different fine motor skill levels.

- Planning and implementing increasingly difficult activities in which small muscles are used.

- Offering children opportunities to learn real skills as well as to explore materials on their own.

- Following up on staff-led projects by providing materials children can explore on their own.

- Providing materials that fit together such as puzzles and Legos, so children can use their fine motor skills.

**Competency Assessment
Module 5: Cognitive**

Your trainer will review records from this observation and others conducted in the last month to assess whether you use skills such as the following:

- Supplying materials that allow children to develop and pursue special talents.

- Offering children space and time to develop and carry out their plans.

- Creating discovery boxes on topics such as magnets, static electricity, solar energy, and weather.

- Offering a wide range of books and magazines that reflect children's diverse interests.

- Providing open-ended materials that children can explore and use in many different ways.

- Providing materials that help children classify, sequence, and understand cause and effect.

- Accepting and respecting children's ideas, suggestions, and solutions.

- Asking recall questions to help children describe what they know, remember the past, and relate the past to the present.

- Asking convergent questions to help children think about cause and effect or to make predictions.

- Asking divergent questions so children can think of several possible ideas or solutions.

- Asking evaluative questions so children learn to make judgments.

- Exposing children to new information, ideas, concepts, and experiences.

- Talking to and questioning children about what they are observing and learning.

- Encouraging children to make decisions and solve problems on their own, without adult assistance.

- Encouraging children's emerging sense of humor by suggesting they write and share riddles, jokes, and limericks.

- Involving children in planning and evaluating the program's routines and activities.

- Planning activities that allow children to explore natural science and the outdoor environment.

- Providing opportunities for children to participate in and learn about the real world.

- Following a schedule that allows children to choose what they want to do and provides enough time for long-term projects.

- Involving children in setting rules and establishing procedures for the program's operations.

- Allowing children plenty of time to talk to each other and to the staff.

- Providing opportunities for children to demonstrate their growing cognitive skills and apply them to new situations.

- Introducing children to the steps in problem solving.

- Providing opportunities for children to learn in ways that match their learning styles.

Competency Assessment
Module 6: Communication

Your trainer will review records from this observation and others conducted in the last month to assess whether you use skills such as the following:

- Arranging the environment so there are places where children can work, play, and talk in small groups.

- Providing materials, time, and space for children to make up their own games and activities.

- Providing props, costumes, and other materials that encourage language development activities such as dramatic play, making up skits, and puppetry.

- Stocking the quiet area with materials that encourage writing—such as pens, pencils, paper, book-binding materials, and a computer, if available.

- Including reading and writing materials in all interest areas.

- Providing (or arranging for use of) audio and video tape equipment so children can record their storytelling, plays, skits, and other creations.

- Including books, magazines, and reference materials in the quiet area in response to children's interests and to expose them to new ideas and topics.

- Designating the quiet area as a place where children can do homework.

- Using printing rather than cursive writing on signs, bulletin boards, and other written materials directed at children.

- Responding to children's requests for assistance.

- Asking open-ended questions to encourage children to think and express their ideas.

- Accepting children's use of slang and popular expressions while serving as a model for standard use of language.

- Supporting children's bilingualism through activities and interactions in the program.

- Reminding children to review the rules before beginning a game or sport so all players can agree on how to play the game and keep score.

- Showing respect for what children have to say.

- Observing children's nonverbal cues and using the cues to ask questions about their ideas and feelings.

- Encouraging children to read and write for pleasure, not only because they must complete assigned work.

- Helping children find the words to express their ideas and feelings.

- Using group meetings as opportunities for children to share their ideas, raise concerns, and discuss solutions.

- Encouraging children to share folklore, oral traditions, stories, songs, and books that reflect their family backgrounds.

- Helping children plan and implement special interest clubs that use or explore communication skills.

- Offering materials and activities that respond to children's individual and developmental skills and interests.

- Keeping in touch with the elementary schools attended by children to find out what materials and activities the program could offer to build on or enrich the experiences offered in school.

- Planning trips and special activities to expand children's language skills and interests.

- Building opportunities for children to develop and use communication skills into all program activities, not just those specifically related to reading, writing, listening, and speaking.

Competency Assessment
Module 7: Creative

Your trainer will review records from this observation and others conducted in the last month to assess whether you use skills such as the following:

- Providing open-ended materials with which children can do many things.

- Arranging the environment so children can spread out, explore, and be messy.

- Providing sufficient storage space for projects and creations that cannot be completed in one day.

- Allowing creations to stay in place for several days so children can continue using them and possibly expand them.

- Following a daily schedule that includes long blocks of time when children are free to organize their own games and activities without adult involvement.

- Providing sufficient time in the daily schedule for children to make plans and carry them out.

- Surrounding children with examples of creative work.

- Storing materials and equipment where children can easily select, replace, and care for them without adult assistance.

- Offering materials that allow children to explore subjects and interests introduced at school or through experiences such as field trips.

- Encouraging children to express their ideas and feelings.

- Offering activities that allow children to develop and carry out their own plans.

- Extending younger children's dramatic play.

- Introducing children to brainstorming so they can use it as a problem-solving tool.

- Planning a variety of activities that introduce children to the visual and expressive arts.

- Helping children develop specific skills they can use in their creative work.

- Responding to children's ideas for projects and activities.

- Avoiding use of coloring books, pre-packaged craft projects, and dittos.

- Valuing the characteristics that make each child a unique individual.

- Helping children understand that it takes hard work and practice to develop their talents.

- Encouraging children to take risks, learn from their mistakes, and try again.

- Inviting children to display or share the results of their creative work.

- Calling attention to sensory experiences.

- Asking a variety of questions that encourage children to think about things in new ways.

- Accepting and valuing each child's unique creative expression.

- Modeling creativity by sharing your interests, taking risks, and solving problems.

Competency Assessment
Module 8: Self

Your trainer will review records from this observation and others conducted in the last month to assess whether you use skills such as the following:

- Observing children to identify what makes them unique and letting them know you value their individuality.

- Listening carefully to children and taking their concerns seriously without interrupting, judging, or giving unasked-for advice.

- Showing children in many ways that you enjoy being with them.

- Letting children know they are cared for by offering gentle physical or nonverbal contact—a hug, a touch, a smile.

- Identifying children's interests through observation, surveys, and conversations; using the information to plan activities and provide materials.

- Knowing what each child is able to do and showing you value each child's unique skills and characteristics.

- Offering a wide variety of activities that do not limit children's options because of individual differences; making no biased remarks.

- Learning words in the native language of children whose first language is not English.

- Working with parents and colleagues to make sure each child receives the individual attention he or she needs.

- Making sure the program's environment and activities help children learn about and appreciate a variety of cultures and ethnic groups.

- Acknowledging children's efforts and accomplishments.

- Encouraging children to take pride in their efforts and accomplishments.

- Reinforcing behavior when it is cooperative, helpful, and shows value for other's accomplishments.

- Offering sports and games that help children learn to value fairness, cooperation, and personal growth.

- Providing opportunities for children to develop leadership skills.

- Helping children deal with setbacks by accepting their feelings and failures and responding respectfully.

- Encouraging children to solve their own problems; intervening only when it seems they can't find a solution or when someone might get hurt.

- Showing children you have a positive relationship with their parents and that their family's involvement is both valued and appreciated.

- Encouraging children to learn through trial and error.

- Involving children in the program's daily operations and weekly chores.

157

- Providing a variety of materials, equipment, and activities to meet a wide range of abilities.

- Allowing children to use their growing independence in safe and age-appropriate ways.

- Providing children with time and resources needed to pursue their interests or to master a skill.

- Allowing children to choose what they want to do and to choose not to participate in an activity.

- Helping children gain the skills they need to complete a task so they can overcome fear of failure.

Competency Assessment
Module 9: Social

Your trainer will review records from this observation and others conducted in the last month to assess whether you use skills such as the following:

- Observing and listening to learn how each child relates to the others in the program.

- Encouraging children to help each other.

- Encouraging children to solve their own conflicts.

- Observing and assisting children who have difficulty being accepted by their peers.

- Providing enough time in the schedule for self-selected activities so children can decide with whom they would like to be.

- Accepting children's need to establish their own identities as they use slang and create a "culture" separate from adults.

- Identifying your own feelings when appropriate to model acceptable ways to express feelings.

- Accepting children's feelings while helping them learn to control their actions.

- Encouraging children to value what makes each person a unique individual.

- Using group meetings to solve problems that involve all the children.

- Modeling positive ways to interact with other people of all ages.

- Planning multi-age activities that encourage cooperation and allow older children to play the role of leader and mentor.

- Involving children in establishing rules that encourage use of social skills.

- Providing a variety of objects and tools that encourage children to explore their world.

- Providing books that help children deal with their feelings about friendship, conflicts, ethnic diversity, and similar topics.

- Providing opportunities for children to belong to groups.

- Offering opportunities for children to be involved in the community.

- Inviting community members to share their special knowledge and skills with the children.

Competency Assessment
Module 10: Guidance

Before the observation period your trainer will assess whether you use skills such as the following:

- Following a daily schedule that allows children to choose their own activities.

- Making sure there are no safety hazards in the environment.

- Storing materials and equipment within children's reach.

- Arranging the environment to encourage appropriate behavior.

Your trainer will review records from this observation and others conducted in the last month to assess whether you use skills such as the following:

- Involving children in setting limits and making rules.

- Involving children in planning activities and selecting materials and equipment.

- Planning some games and activities that encourage cooperation rather than competition.

- Speaking to children with the same tone and respect used with adults.

- Considering the possible reasons for a child's behavior.

- Redirecting children from inappropriate to appropriate activities.

- Giving children opportunities to handle their disagreements without adult assistance.

- Stating directions and reminding children of rules in positive terms.

- Giving genuine praise when children use appropriate behavior.

- Discussing children's misbehavior in private conversations.

- Allowing children to experience the natural and logical consequences of their behavior.

- Offering assistance to children who are out of control.

- Listening to and accepting children's angry feelings while helping them understand the consequences of expressing those feelings inappropriately.

- Talking to children about their day at school, their friends, their concerns, and their feelings.

- Holding group meetings during which children can raise concerns and grievances and work together to solve problems.

- Modeling appropriate ways to express negative feelings.

- Providing creative outlets for expressing strong feelings.

- Working with parents to help a child with a problem express his or her feelings in acceptable ways.

- Teaching children how to use conflict resolution techniques to resolve their differences.

Competency Assessment
Module 11: Families

Before the observation period your trainer will assess whether you use skills such as the following:

- Holding parent-staff conferences to share information about each child's progress and to make plans for the future.

- Using a variety of communication strategies to inform parents about the program.

- Surveying parents' needs and interests and providing appropriate workshops and resources.

- Offering a variety of ways to participate in the program to accommodate parents' varied schedules, skills, and interests.

- Holding regularly scheduled parent meetings and informal family events at times that are convenient for most parents.

- Providing an orientation for new parents so they can get to know staff and learn what children do each day.

- Providing information on child development to help parents understand what behaviors are typical of school-age children.

Your trainer will review records from this observation (either drop-off or pick-up time) and others conducted in the last month to assess whether you use skills such as the following:

- Learning the names of all parents and something about them to build trust.

- Sharing information about yourself with parents to help them get to know you.

- Sharing interesting, positive information about children's activities at the program.

- Encouraging parents to visit the program at any time.

- Letting parents know their contributions are appreciated.

- Suggesting ways to coordinate the child's program and home experiences.

- Asking parents to share information about their child's interests and using this information to individualize the program.

- Responding to parents' questions and concerns.

- Giving parents information about a younger child's routines—for example, that the child didn't eat snack.

- Involving parents in making decisions about their child's activities at the program.

- Maintaining confidentiality about all children and families.

- Working with parents to help them develop their own strategies for handling a difficult behavior.

- Introducing parents to others who live in the same neighborhood or have children of similar ages.

- Making an effort to get to know all the parents in the program.

- Recognizing when parents are under stress and offering additional support.

- Notifying a supervisor when it seems that parents need professional help.

Competency Assessment
Module 12: Families

Your trainer will review records from this observation (including a staff meeting) and others conducted in the last month to assess whether you use skills such as the following:

- Using systematic, objective observation to accurately record what children say and do.

- Observing children in different settings and at different times of the day.

- Conducting observations for specific reasons.

- Recording many instances of a child's actions before drawing conclusions.

- Sharing observation information with parents and encouraging them to help their children grow and develop.

- Developing an observation schedule with colleagues so every child is observed on a regular basis.

- Conducting periodic joint observations to ensure accuracy.

- Participating in regular staff meetings to plan and evaluate the program.

- Discussing observation recordings with colleagues when planning for individuals and for the group.

- Using parent surveys and open-ended questionnaires to collect information about children and to evaluate the program.

- Involving children in planning and evaluating the program.

- Changing aspects of the program to address individual cultures, interests, needs, and abilities.

- Conducting periodic surveys to identify children's interests and to encourage them to evaluate the program.

- Helping children form clubs that allow them to explore their shared interests.

- Appreciating and using the strengths of other team members.

- Coordinating with appropriate resources in the community.

- Using creative thinking skills in planning and problem solving.

- Meeting and talking with colleagues and the supervisor to provide input on program issues.

- Keeping informed about job responsibilities and program policies and procedures.

- Reviewing program policies before starting a new task.

- Completing management tasks according to a schedule.

- Following the program's system for accurate and timely record keeping.

- Providing substitute staff with adequate information on weekly plans and program practices.

- Answering parents' questions about program policies and procedures and referring parents to the supervisor when appropriate.

Appendices

Appendix A

Planning Form for Group Training Sessions

Planning Form for Group Training Sessions

Use this form to plan group sessions for staff working on the same module. You can tailor the agenda to address individual interests and training needs. Ask staff to submit their completed Learning Activities prior to each session for your review and written comments. Return them at the end of the session. Offer to meet with individuals to discuss your feedback.

Module: _____

Overview

I. **Opening** (Ask an open-ended question to promote discussion of the topics addressed in this module.)

_____

_____

_____

II. **Discussion Questions** (Be prepared to lead a discussion on the key points addressed in the module.)

_____

_____

_____

III. Discussion of Overview

A. Review the examples of ways staff demonstrate their competence in this area. Ask staff to give examples of ways they use their skills in each category.

B. Discuss the vignettes, staff responses to the questions, and the answers provided at the end of the module. Ask questions such as:

- How do you feel about the way the staff member handled this situation?
- How would you handle a similar situation in your program?

_____

_____

_____

C. Discuss the section relating personal experiences to the topic of the module (e.g., Your Own Self-Discipline).

IV. Ending the Session

Return completed Overviews and Pre-Training Assessments. Schedule times to meet individually with staff to discuss their responses and the three to five skills and topics they want to learn more about.

Learning Activity _____ *

I. Opening

Begin by asking an open-ended question, reviewing the previous Learning Activity, or discussing a follow-up assignment from the previous meeting.

_____

_____

_____

_____

_____

_____

II. Discussion Questions

Lead a discussion focused on the key points presented in the Learning Activity.

_____

_____

_____

_____

_____

_____

_____

_____

III. Review of Activity

Ask staff to describe their experiences completing this Learning Activity. Encourage them to share examples from their completed activities.

_____

_____

_____

_____

_____

_____

_____

---

* Complete one for each Learning Activity in this module.

170

IV. Additional Resources/Activities

List any materials, audiovisual resources, topics for discussion, or exercises you will use to supplement the Learning Activities.

_____

_____

_____

_____

_____

V. Ending the Session*

- Return completed Learning Activities with your comments. Offer to review and discuss these during individual meetings with interested staff.

- Give a brief overview of the next Learning Activity.

_____

_____

_____

_____

_____

* If this is the last session in the module, discuss **Summarizing Your Progress** before ending the session.

- Have each person share an example of what they learned while working on this module.

- Ask staff to share some of the ways they adapted or changed their practices.
  - How have children responded to the changes?
  - How have parents responded to the changes?

Then schedule individual meetings with staff to administer the Knowledge and Competency Assessments.

Appendix B

Answer Sheets
for
Knowledge Assessments

Module 1: Safe

Total of 100 points possible. Passing score is 80 or above. Note that for questions 6-14, there are many possible correct responses.

Each Answer Worth	Possible Total Points	**Answer**
5	5	**1.** e
5	5	**2.** e
5	5	**3.** e
5	5	**4.** d
5	5	**5.** e

5 ea.   10   **6.** Possible correct responses include:

- Set up interest areas using dividers that are low enough to see all children at all times.
- Place dangerous substances in covered, safe containers and store in locked cabinets.
- Know where to locate and how to use fire extinguishers.
- Secure or remove furniture that could fall or be pulled over.
- Use open shelves, not chests, for storage.
- Store heavy items on the bottom shelves of bookcases or cabinets.
- Include staff assignments in the daily schedule.
- Conduct regular safety checks of materials and equipment.
- Designate separate areas for different kinds of activities.
- Play ball games away from streets.
- Create a floor plan that allows children to move freely from one area to another and provides easy access to exits.

5 ea.   10   **7.** Refer to the indoor safety checklist in Learning Activity I: Creating and Maintaining a Safe Environment (pp. 45-46) for possible correct responses.

5 ea.   10   **8.** Refer to the outdoor safety checklist in Learning Activity I: Creating and Maintaining a Safe Environment (p. 47) for possible correct responses.

5 ea.   10   **9.** Answers may vary, but should include sufficient detail to indicate staff member responded appropriately in the emergency, keeping the children's safety a priority.

5   5   **10.** Response should indicate that school-age children are at an age where they can understand the reasons for doing things. By discussing safety rules with children, staff can explain how and why accidents happen and what children can do to prevent them. Also, if children take an active part in developing safety rules, they are more apt to follow them.

5   5   **11.** Possible correct responses include:

- She will stay calm and try not to panic.
- She will stay where she is if it is an area where there are a lot of people.
- She will remember to give her name and phone number so someone can help her.
- She will try to ask an adult, preferably someone who works at the zoo, to help her locate the group.

Each Answer Worth	Possible Total Points	Answer
5 ea.	10	**12.** Possible correct responses include:

- Inform parents well in advance of the trip and have them sign permission slips.
- Check the first-aid kit and replace missing or outdated items.
- Travel to the site from the program, if possible, and look for potential problems before the actual trip.
- Plan for the unexpected.
- Plan for children in the group to be identified by either special tags or t-shirts.
- Recruit volunteers to help supervise children if the group is large.
- Prepare a trip folder with emergency phone numbers, signed emergency forms, and a list of backup activities.

2-1/2 ea.	5	**13.** Possible correct responses include:

- Involve children in identifying potential problems and hazards and in listing rules.
- Encourage children to remind each other of important rules.
- Have children demonstrate how to use equipment and play games appropriately.
- Ask children to make up safety slogans and posters to help each other remember rules.

10	10	**14.** Answers may vary, but should reflect an understanding that keeping children safe is a priority for all people who care for children.

===

Module 2: Healthy

Total of 100 points possible. Passing score is 80 or above. Note that for questions 5-11, there are many possible correct responses.

Each Answer Worth	Possible Total Points	Answer
5	5	**1.** e
5	5	**2.** e
5	5	**3.** e
5	5	**4.** a
5 ea.	10	**5.** Possible correct responses include:

- Check the environment daily to make sure it is clean and uncluttered.
- Report problems to the supervisor.
- Clean up spills as they happen.
- Store food properly.
- Throw away garbage promptly.
- Keep tissues, paper towels, and soap within children's reach.
- Use a bleach solution to disinfect surfaces, materials, and equipment.
- Follow handwashing procedures recommended by the Centers for Disease Control.
- Conduct informal, daily child health checks.
- Be alert to signs of illness.
- Make sure cots and bedding used by kindergarten children are washed and disinfected weekly.

176

Each Answer Worth	Possible Total Points	Answer
5 ea.	10	**6.** Possible correct responses include: • Difficulty breathing • Yellowish skin or eyes • Feverish appearance • Severe coughing • Unusual skin patches • Unusual behavior
5 ea.	10	**7.** Refer to the contagious diseases chart in Learning Activity I: Maintaining a Hygienic Environment (pp. 107-108) for possible correct responses.
5 ea.	10	**8.** Possible correct responses include: • Having trouble finding something to wear to school • Arguing with a friend • Misplacing homework • Getting ready for a party • Feeling bored • Losing a game
5 ea.	10	**9.** Possible correct responses include: • When offering competitive activities, also offer alternatives. • Anticipate potentially stressful situations and take steps to minimize the stress. • Listen to children and let them know you understand. • Conduct frequent observations in different settings. • Accept and respect each child as an individual. • Encourage children to recognize stress and use stress management techniques. • Arrange the environment so there are places where children can be alone.
10	10	**10.** Response should demonstrate an understanding of sources of short- and long-term stress and healthy strategies children and adults can use to reduce and handle stress.
10	10	**11.** Response should indicate the staff member knows how to follow state laws and local policies for filing reports of suspected child abuse or neglect.
2-1/2 ea.	10	**12.** Match **four** items. a. 2 b. 3 c. 4 d. 1

Module 3: Program Environment

Total of 100 points possible. Passing score is 80 or above. Note that for questions 4-12, there are many possible correct answers.

Each Answer Worth	Possible Total Points	**Answer**
5	5	**1.** e
5	5	**2.** c
5	5	**3.** a
5 ea.	10	**4.** Refer to Learning Activity II: Creating an Indoor Environment (pp. 180-183) for a complete description of interest areas.
5 ea.	10	**5.** Possible correct responses include:

- Will they interest the children?
- Do the children have the skills needed to handle them?
- Will they challenge children to think and explore?
- Do they reflect children's ethnicity?
- Do they show people with disabilities engaged in meaningful tasks?
- Do they help achieve your goals for children?

1 ea.	10	**6.** Possible correct responses include:

    a. <u>Quiet area</u>: writing supplies, books, magazines, computer and software, tape or CD player, tapes or CDs

    b. <u>Dramatic play area</u>: costumes, puppets, props, clothes, materials for making puppets

    c. <u>Math area</u>: beads and laces, paper, pencils, abacus, measuring tapes, calculators, Legos

    d. <u>Blocks and construction area</u>: unit blocks, small cars and trucks, appliance cartons, wood or rubber people and animals, Lincoln logs

    e. <u>Arts and crafts area</u>: paper, paints, brushes, markers, playdough, sponges, oilcloth, easels, collage items, colored chalk, Plaster of Paris

5 ea	10	**7.** Possible correct responses include:

- <u>Dramatic play area</u>: house corner or area dedicated to a special theme (e.g., mini-mall)
- <u>Arts and crafts area</u>: modeling and carving or weaving and stitchery
- <u>Science and nature area</u>: natural science, how things work, or inventions

5 ea.	10	**8.** Possible correct responses include:

- Bring indoor activities outdoors.
- Make a swing from a tractor tire.
- Use cable spools to create climbing or meeting places.
- Provide boxes and planks for children's constructions.
- Gather books of jump rope rhymes.

5	5	**9.** Response should describe how to make transitions pleasant and meaningful for children, rather than times when they have to wait with nothing to do.

Each Answer Worth	Possible Total Points	**Answer**

2 ea.   10   **10**. Possible correct responses include:

<u>5- to 7-years</u>

- Play games—board games, outdoor games, games they make up.
- Use simple tools.
- Read and be read to.
- Play in the house corner.
- Play with puppets.
- Participate in clubs.
- Build with blocks.
- Take care of their own routines.

<u>8- to 10-years</u>

- Write stories and plays.
- Make up jokes and riddles.
- Do brainteasers.
- Play organized games and sports.
- Dance to music—make up dances.
- Play computer games.
- Play musical instruments.
- Do experiments.
- Practice physical skills—doing a cartwheel, dribbling a ball, hitting a ball.

<u>11- to 12-years</u>

- Play sports with increased skills.
- Get involved in community projects.
- Engage in long-term projects.
- Read and teach skills to younger children.
- Help plan program activities and recommend materials.
- Write letters, poems, and short stories.
- Establish and participate in clubs.

1 ea.   10   **11.** Possible correct responses include:

a. <u>Water play</u>: hoses, pails, funnels, sprinkler tops, squeeze bottles, cups, sponges
b. <u>Hot-weather play</u>: hoses, buckets, sprinklers, pools
c. <u>Sand play</u>: sieves, muffin tins, ladles, cookie cutters, gelatin molds, coffee pots
d. <u>Physical play</u>: jump ropes. barrels, safety cones, wagons, roller skates, bats, balls
e. <u>Construction</u>: large cartons and crates, large spools, saw horses, cardboard for "roofing"

5 ea.   10   **12.** Refer to the list of criteria in Learning Activity V: Managing the Day (p. 214) for possible correct responses.

Module 4: Physical

Total of 100 points possible. Passing score is 80 or above. Note that for questions 1-10, there are many possible correct responses.

Each Answer Worth	Possible Total Points	Answer

5 ea.   10

1.   Possible correct responses include:

- Have lots of energy to burn, but can become easily tired.
- Begin to enjoy organized games and sports, but generally are not ready for competition.
- Physical growth slows and weight gain is moderate and even.
- Learn to coordinate large and small muscles, gain perceptual motor coordination.
- Are developing a sense of rhythm.

5 ea.   10

2.   Possible correct responses include:

- Body strength increases.
- Reaction times improve.
- Some become involved in competitive sports.
- May compare their abilities to those of peers.
- Have not yet begun growth spurt and do not have full muscle power.
- Wide variations in muscle strength and physical power.

5 ea.   10

3.   Possible correct responses include:

- May test the limits of their physical skills.
- Girls go through growth spurt at about age 11-1/2 to 12.
- Boys go through growth spurt two years later than girls.
- Girls, and boys who are developing more slowly than peers, may drop out of sports and other physical activities.
- As girls enter puberty may develop increased body fat and decreased size, endurance, and muscle power in comparison to boys.

5 ea.   15

4.   Refer to Learning Activity II: Observing and Planning for Children's Physical Development (pp. 251-256) to score this item.

5   5

5.   An example of a correct response follows:

Movement stations provide opportunities for children to develop and improve specific skills. They can accommodate a wide range of skill levels and children can select what they want to do, at their own pace.

5   5

6.   Responses such as the following would be considered correct:

"If you want to skip your turn for now that's okay. If you like, I can practice with you before the next game."

"It can be difficult to learn a new skill. If you like, I can go over the steps, then pitch you a few balls until you feel more comfortable."

2-1/2 ea.   10

7.   The following is an example of a correct response based on the cooperative game, blanketball.

a.   Cooperation: Children have to work with each other to toss the ball.
b.   Acceptance: Each child holds a part of the blanket and contributes to the game.

180

Each Answer Worth	Possible Total Points	Answer
		c. <u>Involvement</u>: Everyone joins in tossing and catching the ball.
		d. <u>Fun</u>: The game is active, but simple to learn. Children won't feel rejected because they did something "wrong."
10	10	**8.** Response should demonstrate understanding of ways children use their senses to coordinate movements.
10	10	**9.** Response should describe a revised game that involves cooperation, acceptance, involvement, and fun.
5	5	**10.** Refer to Learning Activity IV: Using the Environment to Encourage Fine Motor Skills (pp. 274-277) to score this item.
2 ea.	10	**11.** Match **five** items.

a. 3
b. 5
c. 4
d. 1
e. 2

Module 5: Cognitive

Total of 100 points possible. Passing score is 80 or above. Note that for questions 4-8, there are many correct responses.

Each Answer Worth	Possible Total Points	Answer
1	10	**1.** Match **nine** items. If all are correct, give 10 points.

1. b   4. c   7. a
2. a   5. a   8. c
3. b   6. c   9. b

Each Answer Worth	Possible Total Points	Answer
5	5	**2.** b
5	5	**3.** c
5 ea.	10	**4.** Possible correct responses follow:

a. <u>Why?</u> When children know how to learn they gain self-confidence and develop the skills to explore, try out ideas, solve problems, and take on new challenges.

b. <u>What can you do to help</u>?

- Ask open-ended questions.
- Encourage children to use thinking skills such as classification and sequencing.
- Expose children to new ideas.
- Talk with children about what they are doing.
- Encourage children to make decisions and solve problems.

Each Answer Worth	Possible Total Points	**Answer**

- Accept and respect children's ideas, suggestions, and solutions.
- Provide resources such as dictionaries, atlases, almanacs, and books related to special interests.

2-1/2 ea. **5** **5.** Refer to Learning Activity IV: Using the Physical Environment to Promote Cognitive Development (pp. 328-355) for possible correct responses.

2-1/2 ea. **20** **6.** Possible correct responses for the roller skating example include:

a. <u>Awareness</u>: provide knee and elbow safety pads and a helmet; set aside a safe area for skating; demonstrate how to maintain balance; tell children, "You can do it."

b. <u>Exploration</u>: provide time for children to practice; comment on children's successes; if children fall, ask them to think about what happened just before they fell; encourage children to learn from mistakes.

c. <u>Inquiry</u>: introduce advanced skills, such as skating backwards; encourage children to make up their own techniques; have children teach each other; suggest visiting a roller-skating rink.

d. <u>Utilization</u>: plan a field trip to the roller skating rink; suggest to families that they might rent in-line skates on the weekend; ask children if they'd like to put on a roller skating show—like an ice skating show.

2 ea. **10** **7.** A possible correct response is described below.

a. <u>Gather information</u>. We have three of the same kind of plant. They are all on the window sill. They are all healthy.

b. <u>State the problem clearly</u>. We think that plants need light to grow and stay healthy. We want to know how much light is needed.

c. <u>Generate ideas</u>. We could move some of the plants away from the window and put them under a lamp. We could move some plants away from the window to a shelf across the room. We could leave some on the window sill.

d. <u>Evaluate the answers and select a "best" option</u>. We will try them all.

e. <u>Test out the option</u>. We will leave the plants in their new locations for several weeks, and check how they are doing every week.

2-1/2 ea. **10** **8.** Possible correct responses follow.

a. This question encourages children to evaluate. They might put themselves in the place of the boy in the story and think about what they would do in the same situation. They might review what has happened in the story, then decide what he should do.

b. This question encourages children to think about what they already know. The children can recall what they know about the topic, dinosaurs.

c. This question encourages children to think about cause and effect. They might descibe the conditions that are causing the plants to do well.

d. This question encourages children to come up with possible ideas and solutions. They are asked to use their skills to think of ways to make the field trip special.

182

Each Answer Worth	Possible Total Points	Answer

Each Answer Worth	Possible Total Points	**Answer**
2 ea.	15	**9.** Match **seven** items. Give 2 points for each correct response. If all are correct give 15 points.

a. 3
b. 6
c. 2
d. 7
e. 4
f. 1
g. 5

2-1/2 ea.	10	**10.** Match **four** items.

a. 3
b. 1
c. 2
d. 4

Module 6: Communication

Total of 100 points possible. Passing score is 80 or above. Note that for questions 4-9, there are many possible correct responses.

Each Answer Worth	Possible Total Points	**Answer**
1	10	**1.** Match **nine** items. Give 1 point for each correct response. If all are correct, give 10 points.

1.	b	4.	b	7.	b
2.	a	5.	c	8.	a
3.	c	6.	c	9.	a

5	5	**2.** e
5	5	**3.** e

5 ea.	10	**4.** Possible correct responses include:

a. They encourage the speaker to assume responsibility for his or her feelings rather than blaming someone else.
b. Communication is likely to be more effective and lead to mutually acceptable solutions.
c. They help defuse tense situations.

5 ea.	15	**5.** Possible correct responses include:

- Encourage children to start a Newspaper or Creative Writing Club.
- Encourage children to write and perform plays, skits, and musicals.
- Encourage children to write and share poetry and short stories.
- Suggest that interested children keep journals.
- Help interested children research topics of their own choice.

		• Create message boards.
		• Provide information on pen pals.
		• Stock the quiet area with plenty of paper and pens.
		• Provide tables in the quiet area for doing homework.

5 ea. 10 **6.** Refer to Learning Activity III: Using the Physical Environment to Promote Communication Skills (pp. 388-393) to score this item.

5 ea. 15 **7.** Responses should indicate how the magazines reflect the interests and communication skill levels of the children enrolled.

5 ea. 10 **8.** Possible correct responses include:

- They feel in control of their lives.
- They feel capable.
- They learn how much they really know.
- They extend their thinking and learn more.
- They make sense of the things affecting their lives.
- They express and defend personal opinions.

2-1/2 ea. 20 **9.** Possible correct responses follow.

Children might use <u>listening skills at the program</u> to hear: announcements about daily activities; problem-solving discussions at group meeting; explanation of rules for a game; words to a song; someone else's ideas.

Children might use <u>listening skills at home</u> to hear: family conversations; parents' instructions, praise, and guidance; requests from siblings; a conversation over the phone.

Children might use <u>speaking skills at the program</u> to: express ideas during meetings or conversations; practice for a play; discuss a problem; describe what happened on a field trip; state the rules for a game.

Children might use <u>speaking skills at home</u> to: share ideas or feelings with parents; answer the phone; explain to siblings how they feel; tell family members about school activities; practice a speech for a homework assignment.

Children might use <u>reading skills at the program</u> to read: notices on the bulletin board; a label on a shelf; minutes of a meeting; books and journals; another child's poem or short story; instructions for an experiment or craft project.

Children might use <u>reading skills at home</u> to read: a newspaper or magazine; a homework assignment; a recipe in a cookbook; a message from parents; to a younger sibling; a community newsletter.

Children might use <u>writing skills at the program</u> to write: an idea for the suggestion box; rules to a game they made up; a poem or short story; a sign for the bulletin board; homework; a play or skit; messages to each other.

Children might use <u>writing skills at home</u> to write: a message to a family member; homework; a thank you letter to a relative; a letter to a pen pal; a grocery list; a birthday wish list; the answers to a crossword puzzle.

Module 7: Creative

Total of 100 points possible. Passing score is 80 or above. Note that for questions 4-9, there are many possible correct responses.

Each Answer Worth	Possible Total Points	Answer
5	5	**1.** e
5	5	**2.** b
5	5	**3.** c

4. (10 / 10) An example of a correct response follows:

> Ms. Jensen needs to be flexible. She should support the children's interests by telling them where they can find some paper and drawing materials.

5. (5 ea. / 10) Possible correct responses include:

- There are large blocks of time during which children can choose what they want to do and with whom.
- Most planned activities are voluntary.
- There are a wide variety of materials and activities in accordance with the range of children's interests and ages.
- Children are exposed to the arts and aesthetic experiences.
- Staff serve as facilitators rather than directors.
- Children can make messes and mistakes.
- Staff allow children to be different and help them value their own uniqueness and that of others.
- Staff identify sources of stress and make changes to reduce stress and anxiety.

6. (10 / 10) Refer to Learning Activity III: Supporting Children's Long-Term Projects (pp. 33-39) to score this item.

7. (2-1/2 / 10) Possible open-ended materials include:

- Clay and playdough
- Large sheet or tablecloth
- Sewing items and fabrics
- Wood scraps
- Blocks
- A clock or a machine and tools to take the object apart
- Cardboard, tape, markers, and other supplies for making games
- Computer drawing program
- Props for plays and dramatic play

Refer to Learning Activity V: Filling the Environment with Open-Ended Materials That Promote Creativity (pp. 53-61) for examples of ways children <u>use</u> open-ended materials.

8. (5 / 5) Response should demonstrate how staff member was original, resourceful, innovative, solved a problem, and/or created something that is personally meaningful.

185

Each Answer Worth	Possible Total Points	Answer
5	20	**9.** Possible correct responses include:

- Follow a schedule with long blocks of time when Yancey can choose what to do.
- Include resources on training animals in the quiet area.
- Suggest he start a club with others who share his interest.
- Invite a veterinarian to give a presentation at the program.
- Encourage him to draw or write about his interest.

Each Answer Worth	Possible Total Points	Answer
2 ea.	10	**10.** Statements b, d, and g are true. Statements a, c, e, f, and h are false
2-1/2 ea.	10	**11.** Match **four** items.

a. 4
b. 2
c. 3
d. 1

Module 8: Self

Total of 100 points possible. Passing score is 80 or above. Note that for questions 1-6 and 11, there are many possible correct answers.

Each Answer Worth	Possible Total Points	Answer
5 ea.	15	**1.** Possible correct responses include:

- Show children you appreciate, value, and enjoy being with them.
- Listen to children as they express their feelings and take their concerns seriously.
- Observe children often to get to know them.
- Help children learn about and appreciate their own and other cultures.
- Involve children in program operations.
- Seek children's ideas for program materials and activities.
- Encourage children to solve their own problems.

Each Answer Worth	Possible Total Points	Answer
2-1/2 ea.	10	**2.** Refer to Learning Activity V: Promoting Children's Sense of Competence (pp. 108-111) to score this item.
5 ea.	10	**3.** Possible correct responses include:

- Provide the kind and level of support that individual children need.
- Provide furniture and equipment that is the right size for school-age children.
- Store materials and equipment where children can reach them.
- Offer a self-service snack.
- Provide materials, equipment, and activities to meet a wide range of skills and interests.
- Observe frequently, note children's growth and development and make adjustments as needed in the schedule, environment, rules, and activities.

Each Answer Worth	Possible Total Points	Answer
5 ea.	15	**4.** Use your own judgment to determine if a staff member's responses show that he or she knows how to talk to children in ways that foster self-esteem. Possible correct responses follow:

186

Each Answer Worth	Possible Total Points	**Answer**

a. "Todd, would you like some help? You may need to make more than one trip when you have a lot to carry."

b. "Kwami, fighting is not allowed at the school-age program. I'm available to meet with you and Dennis to help you solve your disagreement."

c. "You and your sister Yvonne each have unique talents and ways to do things."

5 ea.	10	**5.** Possible correct responses include:

- Play games to help children learn to value fairness, cooperation, and personal growth.
- Give genuine praise and recognition for children's efforts and accomplishments.
- Encourage children to see their own progress.
- Praise yourself for personal efforts and accomplishments.
- Demonstrate respect for each child's unique characteristics.

5	5	**6.** Response should demonstrate appreciation for oneself.
5	5	**7.** Correct responses: observe, watch, listen to, or talk with.
5	5	**8.** e
2-1/2 ea.	10	**9.** Statements a, b, d, g, and i are true. Statements c, e, f, h, and j are false.
2-1/2 ea.	10	**10.** Match **four** items.

a. 4
b. 1
c. 3
d. 2

5 ea.	5	**11.** Answers will vary but should show how staff member's self-esteem/self-awareness affects his or her relationships with the children.

Module 9: Social

Total of 100 points possible. Passing score is 80 or above. Note that for questions 2-8, there are many possible correct answers.

Each Answer Worth	Possible Total Points	**Answer**
1 ea.	10	**1.** Match **nine** items. Give 1 point for each correct response. If all are correct, give 10 points.

1. b	4. c	7. a
2. a	5. c	8. b
3. b	6. a	9. c

Each Answer Worth	Possible Total Points	Answer

5 ea.   15   2. Possible correct responses include:

- <u>Security and the ability to look, listen, and be calm</u>. Children who have accomplished this milestone can listen to instructions and focus on tasks without being easily distracted.
- <u>Relating: the ability to feel warm and close to others</u>. Children who have accomplished this milestone can work independently and easily join a group at play.
- <u>Intentional two-way communication without words</u>. Children who have accomplished this milestone can observe nonverbal cues and accurately determine what others are communicating.
- <u>Emotional ideas</u>. Children who have accomplished this milestone can use words to express their ideas and feelings.
- <u>Emotional thinking</u>. Children who have accomplished this milestone understand cause-and-effect thinking, predict the consequences of their actions, and set aside immediate gratification for future rewards.

10   10   3. Refer to Learning Activity II: Promoting Children's Play (pp. 145-146) to score this item.

4 ea.   20   4. Possible correct responses include:

- <u>One-on-one time</u>: staff member gives a child individual attention while walking across the field to start a softball game.
- <u>Problem-solving time</u>: staff member asks a child to talk over a problem before choosing an activity for the afternoon.
- <u>Identifying and empathizing with a child's point of view</u>: staff member asks probing questions to gain an understanding of the reasons for a child's behavior.
- <u>Breaking the challenge into small pieces</u>: staff member helps a child develop a step-by-step plan for a difficult project.
- <u>Setting limits</u>: staff member reviews the rules for field trips before arriving at the site.

5 ea.   10   5. Possible correct responses include:

- Establish a warm and supportive connection with the child.
- Use information from observations to talk with the child about things he or she likes to do.
- Plan situations or activities that the child likes.
- Encourage more socially competent children to involve the shy child in an activity.
- Reassure the child that it is okay to play alone if he or she wants to, but also suggest that it may be fun to play or talk with the other children.

5 ea.   10   6. Refer to Learning Activity V: Building a Sense of Community (pp. 169-173) to score this item.

10   10   7. Possible correct responses include:

- Encourage Davida to discuss her feelings about being rejected.
- Take Davida aside and suggest questions she could ask the children to find out what they are doing before trying to join in.

Each Answer Worth	Possible Total Points	**Answer**
		• Take Davida aside and explain the group's accepted social practices for joining in an activity that is already taking place.
		• Help Davida figure out a way to join the jump rope group without taking over—perhaps other children could also join the group so two sets of jumpers could jump at the same time.
10	10	**8.** Descriptions will vary depending on program practices. Possible correct responses would include the following information:
		• Times of meeting.
		• Where to sit.
		• How to be recognized if you want to speak.
		• Importance of using polite behaviors, such as remaining quiet when others are speaking and leaving the meeting without disrupting others.
		• Importance of accepting other people's ideas and suggestions.
		• Allowing people to pass if they don't want to speak.
2-1/2 ea.	5	**9.** Statements a and d are true. Statements b and c are false.

Module 10: Guidance

Total of 100 points possible. Passing score is 80 or above. Note that for questions 5-9, there are many possible correct responses.

Each Answer Worth	Possible Total Points	**Answer**
5	5	**1.** a
5	5	**2.** e
5	5	**3.** e
5	5	**4.** e
3 ea.	15	**5.** An example of a correct response follows:

Problem or conflict: The older children want to play volleyball alone. The younger ones keep trying to play with them.

Stop: The game stops so everyone can regain composure and discuss the situation.

Identify: The children talk about why they are upset. The older children say they want to play alone because the younger ones don't know the rules. The younger ones say they want to learn the rules so they can play too.

Generate: The children think of several possible solutions. At this point, none are rejected.

Evaluate: The children discuss each solution and think about whether it would work, is fair, and what might happen if they tried it. They select an idea to try: offering a sports clinic so the younger children can learn the rules and practice skills such as serving the ball.

Plan: The children discuss how to run a clinic and ask for help from the staff.

Each Answer Worth	Possible Total Points	**Answer**

5 ea.   **10**

6. Examples of correct responses follow:

- Help children use problem-solving skills to develop solutions.
- Talk with children privately, away from the group.
- Help children understand the consequences of their actions and make amends.
- Assume the role of authority only when necessary—but do so firmly.
- Intervene in children's conflicts only when necessary to prevent injuries.
- Maintain appropriate expectations for children's behavior.
- Involve children in setting rules and limits.
- Gain control of your own feelings before disciplining a child. Ask for help from a colleague if needed.

10   **10**

7. Punishment means controlling children's behavior through fear. Discipline means guiding and directing children toward acceptable behavior.

10   **10**

8. The procedure for mediation includes these steps:

- Each child tells his or her side of the story without interruption.
- Each child describes the problem, then what happened in the conflict.
- If the problem still exists, children develop possible solutions.
- If the problem no longer exists, children discuss ways to solve the problem other than the one they chose.

2-1/2 ea.   **20**

9. Possible correct responses include:

a. Tara and Carlos
Possible Cause: The program rules don't acknowledge the older children's independence and ability to behave responsibly.
How Staff Could Respond: Meet with the children to discuss the rules and revise as needed to reflect children's growth and maturity.

b. Josie and Kahil
Possible Cause: The children need more time to make the transition from the program to home.
How Staff Could Respond: Give ten- and five-minute warnings make sure shelves are clearly labeled, praise children for cleaning up, work with children until they clean up without resistance.

c. Ruth
Possible Cause: Ruth is shy or has not yet observed an activity that interests her.
How Staff Could Respond: Get to know Ruth, find out her interests, plan an activity to involve her and another child who has a similar interest.

d. Victor
Possible Cause: The activities and materials do not match Victor's skills and interests.
How Staff Could Respond: Observe and interview Victor to get to know his interests and what he can do. Add materials that are either more or less challenging and that reflect his interests.

Each Answer Worth	Possible Total Points	Answer
2 ea.	10	**10.** Match **five** items.
		a. 5
		b. 1
		c. 2
		d. 4
		e. 3
1 ea.	5	**11.** Statements a, d, and e are true. Statements b and c are false.

Module 11: Families

Total of 100 points possible. Passing score is 80 or above. Note that for questions 1-9, there are many possible correct responses.

5 ea.   10   **1.** Possible correct responses include:

- Hold orientations for new parents several times a year.
- Involve parents in ongoing projects.
- Invite parents to share their interests and talents.
- Hold a family movie night.
- Schedule a "fix-it" night or Saturday.
- Open the program for an evening or a weekend afternoon.
- Ask a parent to organize a program photo album.
- Organize a series of workshops for parents.

2-1/2 ea.   20   **2.** Possible correct responses include:

Parents

- Health and growth history
- Food allergies
- The child's fears
- The family's lifestyle
- The child's reaction when things aren't going well

Staff

- Favorite materials and activities
- How the child plays with others
- What challenges the child enjoys
- How the child reacts to changes in the environment
- What the child talks about while at the program

5   5   **3.** Possible correct responses include:

- Message center
- Parent bulletin board
- Family events
- Program newsletter
- Conversations at drop-off and pick-up times
- Parent handbooks

Each Answer Worth	Possible Total Points	**Answer**

5 ea.   10

4. Possible correct responses include:

<u>Prepare for Conference</u>

- Ask parents what time would be convenient.
- Let parents know the purpose of the conference.
- Ask parents to think of questions they might have and topics they would like to discuss—provide planning form for parents if you have one.
- Review and organize observation notes.
- Review and organize anecdotal records.
- Ask colleagues to share information.
- Collect samples of child's work (e.g., drawings, projects).
- Complete a planning form.
- Role-play with a colleague.

<u>Conduct Conference</u>

- Establish a relaxed and comfortable tone—about five minutes of social conversation.
- Explain how the conference will proceed.
- Provide many opportunities for parents to ask questions and provide input.
- Discuss all areas of child's development.
- Listen carefully and pay attention to parent's reactions.
- Jointly set goals and develop strategies for supporting child's growth and learning at home and at program. (Include older children in planning.)
- Jointly decide how to share goals and strategies with child (if not at conference).
- Begin and end with positive statement about your relationship with child.
- Summarize the discussion.

5 ea.   10

5. Possible correct responses include:

- Lack of sleep
- Illness
- Death of a family member
- Separation and divorce
- An unplanned or unwanted pregnancy
- Failure to receive a promotion
- Extended travel
- Geographic or social isolation

5 ea.   10

6. Possible correct responses include:

- Develop a parent exchange list.
- Post notices of special programs.
- Display books on topics of interest to parents, invite them to borrow them.
- Tell parents about services offered by social services organizations.
- Provide complete information when suggesting a program or event.
- Offer to help reluctant parents contact community resources.
- Call attention to relevant newspaper or magazine articles, television or radio shows, and workshops.

5 ea.   10

7. Possible correct responses include:

- Communicate as often as possible with parents by any effective means.
- Talk to parents about their concerns about their child.

Each Answer Worth	Possible Total Points	**Answer**

- Try to accommodate parents' suggestions related to their children.
- Help parents focus on their child's accomplishments rather than comparing the child to others.
- Show children you respect their families.
- Wait until you are asked before offering advice.
- Share problems with parents when you need to work together to help a child.
- Acknowledge events and transitions in the child's and parents' lives.
- Be sensitive to normal guilt feelings parents may have about the time children spend at the program.
- Keep in touch with the family when a child is absent or ill.
- Help families cope when one parent is away.

Each Answer Worth	Possible Total Points	**Answer**
1 ea.	5	**8.** Refer to Learning Activity II: Keeping Parents Informed About the Program (pp. 276-278) for a complete list of topics to include in a parent handbook.
10	10	**9.** Answer should demonstrate respect and thoughtfulness for parents.
2 ea.	10	**10.** Statements a and c are true. Statements b, d, and e are false.

Module 12: Program Management

Total of 100 points possible. Passing score is 80 or above. Note that for questions 4-11, there are many possible correct responses.

Each Answer Worth	Possible Total Points	**Answer**
5	5	**1.** e
5	5	**2.** c
5	5	**3.** Planning steps include: consulting with the child, family, teacher, and specialist, and gathering resources.
5 ea.	10	**4.** Possible correct responses include:

- To plan a program that reflects children's skills and interests.
- To determine individual children's needs, interests, and strengths.
- To measure each child's progress.
- To develop a strategy for dealing with a challenging behavior.
- To collect information to share with parents or colleagues.
- To evaluate an activity, the environment, a material, or a piece of equipment.

Each Answer Worth	Possible Total Points	**Answer**
10	10	**5.** Response should demonstrate staff member addressed individual skills, needs, and/or interests by changing or adding materials, planning an activity, or tailoring interactions with the child or children.

Each Answer Worth	Possible Total Points	**Answer**
10	10	**6.** Possible correct responses include:

- What do you like best about the program?
- In what ways does the program respond to your child's interests?
- In what ways does the program not meet your child's needs?
- What would you like to change about the program, if anything?

Each Answer Worth	Possible Total Points	**Answer**
5 ea.	10	**7.** Possible correct responses include:

- Special focus
- Meetings
- Special activities
- Outdoor activities
- Changes to the environment
- Target children
- Staff responsibilities

Each Answer Worth	Possible Total Points	**Answer**
10	10	**8.** Refer to Learning Activity II: Individualizing the Program (p. 339) to score this item.
5 ea.	10	**9.** Refer to Learning Activity V: Following Administrative Policies and Procedures (pp. 362-364) to score this item.
5 ea.	10	**10.** Possible correct responses include:

- Ask older children to help administer surveys to learn children's interests.
- Involve children in planning and holding clubs.
- Talk to and listen to children to learn about their interests and ideas.
- Use group meetings as times when children can offer input.
- Hold a weekly Planning Club for interested children.

Each Answer Worth	Possible Total Points	**Answer**
5 ea.	10	**11.** Possible correct responses include:

- Write what you see, not what you think is happening.
- Jot notes frequently. Carry a pad or index cards and pencil.
- Use short phrases.
- Describe *how* a child is doing or saying something.
- Develop an abbreviation system.
- Diagram the environment.
- Underline words to indicate intensity.
- Observe daily, even if only for 5 or 10 minutes.

Each Answer Worth	Possible Total Points	**Answer**
1 ea.	5	**12.** Statements b, c, and e are true. Statements a and d are false.

Module 13: Professionalism

Total of 100 points possible. Passing score is 80 or above. Note that for questions 1-9, there are many possible correct responses.

10	10	**1.**	Answers should make positive statements about being a school-age professional.
10	10	**2.**	Possible correct responses include:

- There are always new developments in the field.
- Continued learning makes people more interesting, active, and able to bring new ideas to the job.
- The staff member cares about children and wants to provide the best possible program.
- The staff member wants to grow professionally, take on more responsibility, advance in the profession, and earn a higher salary.

5 ea.	10	**3.**	Possible correct responses include:

- Join professional organizations.
- Read books and articles.
- Network with other professionals.
- Observe colleagues in action.
- Take advantage of training opportunities.

5 ea.	10	**4.**	Refer to Learning Activity III: Applying Professional Ethics at All Times (pp. 410-412) to score this item.
10	10	**5.**	An advocate for children and families is a person who works for change by speaking out on issues that affect children and families or that affect the working conditions of professionals who work with children.
5 ea.	10	**6.**	Possible correct responses include:

- Share ideas with other professionals and parents.
- Explain practices and children's developmental stages to parents.
- Help parents recognize what children gain from recreational sports and leisure activities.
- Establish and/or participate in organizations of school-age professionals.
- Write a letter to the editor of your local newspaper.
- Encourage others to join professional groups.
- Write to legislators about pending issues.
- Go with a friend to community meetings.
- Volunteer to represent your professional group on a coalition.
- Work and learn with others.
- Volunteer to speak at a school board meeting about professional standards for school-age programs

2-1/2 ea.	20	**7.**	Answer should reflect the content of this module, as well as what the staff member has learned in other modules.
2-1/2 ea.	5	**8.**	Use your own judgment to score this question.
10	10	**9.**	The following is an example of a correct response.

Mr. Cannon should walk over to the softball game and signal to Ms. Diamond to step aside from the children for a minute. When they are out of children's hearing, he should remind her of the program's rules about smoking in front of the children and ask her to put out the cigarette.

2-1/2 ea.	5	**10.**	Statements a and d are true. Statements b, c, and e are false.

Appendix C

Trainer Observation Forms for Competency Assessments

MODULE 1: SAFE*

Staff Member: _____   **Observer:** _____

Date/time: _____   **Setting:** _____

Observation Record: _____

_____

_____

_____

_____

_____

_____

_____

_____

_____

_____

_____

_____

_____

_____

_____

_____

* This Competency Assessment must include observation of an emergency drill.

MODULE 1: SAFE (continued)

MODULE 1: SAFE (continued)

Prior to the observation period, assess the following criteria.

The Competent Staff Member Will:

Conduct safety checks (daily and monthly, indoor and outdoor); remove or repair unsafe items; keep safety equipment in good condition; and maintain first-aid and safety supplies.
[ ] met   [ ] partially met   [ ] not met

Check daily to see that equipment and supplies are cleaned up and stored appropriately.
[ ] met   [ ] partially met   [ ] not met

Arrange the program space so there are clear traffic paths and exits.
[ ] met   [ ] partially met   [ ] not met

Designate separate areas for quiet and active play to avoid congestion and collisions.
[ ] met   [ ] partially met   [ ] not met

Arrange the environment so that children and staff are visible at all times.
[ ] met   [ ] partially met   [ ] not met

Make sure there is an accessible telephone in working order.
[ ] met   [ ] partially met   [ ] not met

Limit access to supplies and equipment for children who do not yet have the skills and judgment to use them safely.
[ ] met   [ ] partially met   [ ] not met

Develop and post accident and emergency procedures.
[ ] met   [ ] partially met   [ ] not met

State the correct procedures to follow when there is an accident or emergency.
[ ] met   [ ] partially met   [ ] not met

Maintain up-to-date emergency telephone numbers for all parents.
[ ] met   [ ] partially met   [ ] not met

Monitor children's arrivals and departures.
[ ] met   [ ] partially met   [ ] not met

Invite community representatives to talk with children about safety.
[ ] met   [ ] partially met   [ ] not met

Review your records from this observation and others conducted in the last month; score each criterion of competence that you can substantiate.

The Competent Staff Member Will:

Protect and reassure children while conducting an emergency drill according to established procedures.
[ ] met   [ ] partially met   [ ] not met

Respond quickly and calmly to children in distress.
[ ] met   [ ] partially met   [ ] not met

Intervene immediately when children are involved in unsafe play.
[ ] met   [ ] partially met   [ ] not met

Maintain appropriate child-adult ratios and group sizes.
[ ] met   [ ] partially met   [ ] not met

Plan a daily schedule to include active and quiet play.
[ ] met   [ ] partially met   [ ] not met

Involve children in making the program's safety rules.
[ ] met   [ ] partially met   [ ] not met

Explain rules and procedures for sports and games before play begins.
[ ] met   [ ] partially met   [ ] not met

MODULE 1: SAFE (continued)	
The Competent Staff Member Will:	
Teach children proper procedures for using, cleaning up, and storing equipment and supplies. [ ] met [ ] partially met [ ] not met	Teach children to observe safety rules when away from the program. [ ] met [ ] partially met [ ] not met
Model ways to take risks. [ ] met [ ] partially met [ ] not met	Remind children of safety rules and encourage them to remind each other. [ ] met [ ] partially met [ ] not met
Talk calmly with children about potential hazards in the environment. [ ] met [ ] partially met [ ] not met	Change activities when children are too excited, angry, or tired to play safely. [ ] met [ ] partially met [ ] not met

MODULE 2: HEALTHY

Page 1

Staff Member: _____   Observer: _____

Date/time: _____   Setting: _____

Observation Record: _____

_____

_____

_____

_____

_____

_____

_____

_____

_____

_____

_____

_____

_____

_____

203

MODULE 2: HEALTHY (continued)

MODULE 2: HEALTHY (continued)

Prior to the observation period, assess the following criteria.

The Competent Staff Member Will:

Check the facility daily for adequate ventilation and lighting, comfortable room temperature, and good sanitation.
[ ] met   [ ] partially met   [ ] not met

Place tissues, paper towels, and soap within children's reach.
[ ] met   [ ] partially met   [ ] not met

Provide resources on health and hygiene.
[ ] met   [ ] partially met   [ ] not met

Keep a supply of sanitary pads and tampons in the girls' bathroom and make sure girls know where these items are.
[ ] met   [ ] partially met   [ ] not met

State the program regulations and state laws related to reporting child abuse and neglect, and describe the signs of possible child maltreatment.
[ ] met   [ ] partially met   [ ] not met

State the symptoms of common childhood illnesses, syndromes, and progressive diseases.
[ ] met   [ ] partially met   [ ] not met

Review your records from this observation and others conducted in the last month; score each criterion of competence that you can substantiate.

The Competent Staff Member Will:

Open windows daily to let in fresh air (if needed during observation period).
[ ] met   [ ] partially met   [ ] not met

Clean and disinfect surfaces before using for food preparation.
[ ] met   [ ] partially met   [ ] not met

Wash hands and encourage children to wash theirs using techniques recommended by the Centers for Disease Control.
[ ] met   [ ] partially met   [ ] not met

Complete daily health checks and observe children for signs of illness.
[ ] met   [ ] partially met   [ ] not met

Provide opportunities for children to plan, prepare, and serve meals and snacks.
[ ] met   [ ] partially met   [ ] not met

Offer self-service snack so children can determine when, what, and how much to eat.
[ ] met   [ ] partially met   [ ] not met

Serve "family-style" meals and eat with children in a relaxing manner.
[ ] met   [ ] partially met   [ ] not met

Encourage children to drink water and take breaks when exercising or outdoors on hot days.
[ ] met   [ ] partially met   [ ] not met

Model habits that promote good health and nutrition.
[ ] met   [ ] partially met   [ ] not met

Maintain a positive, relaxed, and pleasant program atmosphere to reduce tension and stress.
[ ] met   [ ] partially met   [ ] not met

Help children learn ways to recognize, reduce, and cope with stress.
[ ] met   [ ] partially met   [ ] not met

Use a flexible schedule so children can go outdoors, rest, relax, be active, and eat as needed.
[ ] met   [ ] partially met   [ ] not met

Be alert to changes in children's behavior that may signal abuse or neglect.
[ ] met   [ ] partially met   [ ] not met

Support families and help them get the services they need.
[ ] met   [ ] partially met   [ ] not met

MODULE 3: PROGRAM ENVIRONMENT

Page 1

Staff Member: _____

Observer: _____

Date/time: _____

Setting: _____

Observation Record: _____

206

MODULE 3: PROGRAM ENVIRONMENT (continued)

Page 2

207

MODULE 3: PROGRAM ENVIRONMENT (continued)

Prior to the observation period, assess the following criteria:

The Competent Staff Member Will:

Create a variety of well-equipped, indoor and outdoor interest areas that reflect children's skills and interests.
[ ] met   [ ] partially met   [ ] not met

Rotate interest areas or create sub-areas in response to changing skills and interests.
[ ] met   [ ] partially met   [ ] not met

Provide sufficient space and appropriate equipment for group games and sports, indoors and outdoors.
[ ] met   [ ] partially met   [ ] not met

Locate interest areas near resources (such as light and water) used in the area.
[ ] met   [ ] partially met   [ ] not met

Define separate spaces, indoors and outdoors, for active and quiet play.
[ ] met   [ ] partially met   [ ] not met

Store materials on low, open shelves and storage units so they can be easily selected and replaced.
[ ] met   [ ] partially met   [ ] not met

Provide materials that reflect diversity and show no bias.
[ ] met   [ ] partially met   [ ] not met

Provide sufficient space for children to safely store their belongings, long-term projects, and works in progress.
[ ] met   [ ] partially met   [ ] not met

Create soft and cozy areas where children can play alone, read, listen to music, daydream, or talk with a friend.
[ ] met   [ ] partially met   [ ] not met

Adapt the environment, if necessary, to make it appropriate for children with special needs.
[ ] met   [ ] partially met   [ ] not met

Arrange the outdoor area to support a variety of activities.
[ ] met   [ ] partially met   [ ] not met

Help older children create spaces designated for their use only.
[ ] met   [ ] partially met   [ ] not met

Review your records from this observation and others conducted in the last month; score each criterion of competence that you can substantiate.

The Competent Staff Member Will:

Involve children when arranging and rearranging the space used by the program.
[ ] met   [ ] partially met   [ ] not met

Offer a variety of open-ended materials and equipment children can use in different ways.
[ ] met   [ ] partially met   [ ] not met

Offer a variety of materials and equipment to meet a wide range of skills.
[ ] met   [ ] partially met   [ ] not met

Observe, talk with, listen to, and survey children to determine their interests.
[ ] met   [ ] partially met   [ ] not met

Provide materials that build on interests children develop outside the program.
[ ] met   [ ] partially met   [ ] not met

Follow a schedule that includes long blocks of time when children can choose what they want to do.
[ ] met   [ ] partially met   [ ] not met

MODULE 3: PROGRAM ENVIRONMENT (continued)

The Competent Staff Member Will:

Provide sufficient time in the schedule for children to carry out their plans and do long-term projects.
[ ] met   [ ] partially met   [ ] not met

Offer a balance of activity choices (active and quiet; indoor and outdoor; individual, small group, and large group).
[ ] met   [ ] partially met   [ ] not met

Schedule time for children to nap or rest after morning kindergarten.
[ ] met   [ ] partially met   [ ] not met

Include sufficient time for clean-up at the end of morning, afternoon, and full-day sessions.
[ ] met   [ ] partially met   [ ] not met

Allow children to meet their personal needs on individual schedules.
[ ] met   [ ] partially met   [ ] not met

Manage transitions so children do not have to wait with nothing to do.
[ ] met   [ ] partially met   [ ] not met

209

MODULE 4: PHYSICAL

Staff Member: _____

Date/time: _____

Observation Record: _____

Observer: _____

Setting: _____

Page 1

MODULE 4: PHYSICAL (continued)

211

MODULE 4: PHYSICAL (continued)

Review your records from this observation and others conducted in the last month; score each criterion of competence that you can substantiate.

The Competent Staff Member Will:

Provide space and time for children to engage in active play every day.
[ ] met   [ ] partially met   [ ] not met

Encourage children when they are learning new skills and provide assistance upon request.
[ ] met   [ ] partially met   [ ] not met

Suggest ways children can coordinate movement of their large and small muscles.
[ ] met   [ ] partially met   [ ] not met

Help children develop an awareness of rhythm so they can coordinate their movements.
[ ] met   [ ] partially met   [ ] not met

Observe and record information about each child's physical strengths, interests, and needs.
[ ] met   [ ] partially met   [ ] not met

Provide a variety of materials and activities to challenge a wide range of physical capabilities.
[ ] met   [ ] partially met   [ ] not met

Introduce children to games and activities that encourage physical development and cooperation.
[ ] met   [ ] partially met   [ ] not met

Encourage children to make up and organize their own games.
[ ] met   [ ] partially met   [ ] not met

Encourage children to use their large muscles in daily routines.
[ ] met   [ ] partially met   [ ] not met

Plan and implement increasingly difficult activities in which large muscles are used and that promote development of physical skills used in sports and games.
[ ] met   [ ] partially met   [ ] not met

Provide activities, materials, and equipment that allow all children to develop and maintain physical fitness.
[ ] met   [ ] partially met   [ ] not met

Make sure that children take breaks from vigorous activity and drink plenty of water to prevent dehydration.
[ ] met   [ ] partially met   [ ] not met

Introduce new games and activities regularly so children learn different ways to use their muscles.
[ ] met   [ ] partially met   [ ] not met

Encourage children to keep track of their own progress, rather than comparing themselves to others.
[ ] met   [ ] partially met   [ ] not met

Provide activities, materials, and equipment that accommodate different fine motor skill levels.
[ ] met   [ ] partially met   [ ] not met

Plan and implement increasingly difficult activities in which small muscles are used.
[ ] met   [ ] partially met   [ ] not met

MODULE 4: PHYSICAL (continued)

The Competent Staff Member Will:

Offer children opportunities to learn real skills as well as to explore materials on their own.

[ ] met   [ ] partially met   [ ] not met

Follow up on staff-led projects by providing materials children can explore on their own.

[ ] met   [ ] partially met   [ ] not met

Provide materials that fit together such as puzzles and Legos, so children can use their fine motor skills.

[ ] met   [ ] partially met   [ ] not met

MODULE 5: COGNITIVE

Staff Member: _____   Observer: _____

Date/time: _____   Setting: _____

Observation Record: _____

MODULE 5: COGNITIVE (continued)

MODULE 5: COGNITIVE (continued)

Review your records from this observation and others conducted in the last month; score each criterion of competence that you can substantiate.

The Competent Staff Member Will:

Supply materials that allow children to develop and pursue special talents.
[ ] met   [ ] partially met   [ ] not met

Offer children space and time to develop and carry out their plans.
[ ] met   [ ] partially met   [ ] not met

Create discovery boxes on topics such as magnets, static electricity, solar energy, and weather.
[ ] met   [ ] partially met   [ ] not met

Offer a wide range of books and magazines that reflect children's diverse interests.
[ ] met   [ ] partially met   [ ] not met

Provide open-ended materials that children can explore and use in many different ways.
[ ] met   [ ] partially met   [ ] not met

Provide materials that help children classify, sequence, and understand cause and effect.
[ ] met   [ ] partially met   [ ] not met

Accept and respect children's ideas, suggestions, and solutions.
[ ] met   [ ] partially met   [ ] not met

Ask recall questions to help children describe what they know, remember the past, and relate the past to the present.
[ ] met   [ ] partially met   [ ] not met

Ask convergent questions to help children think about cause and effect or to make predictions.
[ ] met   [ ] partially met   [ ] not met

Ask divergent questions so children can think of several possible ideas or solutions.
[ ] met   [ ] partially met   [ ] not met

Ask evaluative questions so children learn to make judgments.
[ ] met   [ ] partially met   [ ] not met

Expose children to new information, ideas, concepts, and experiences.
[ ] met   [ ] partially met   [ ] not met

Talk to and question children about what they are observing and learning.
[ ] met   [ ] partially met   [ ] not met

Encourage children to make decisions and solve problems on their own, without adult assistance.
[ ] met   [ ] partially met   [ ] not met

Encourage children's emerging sense of humor by suggesting they write and share riddles, jokes, and limericks.
[ ] met   [ ] partially met   [ ] not met

Involve children in planning and evaluating the program's routines and activities.
[ ] met   [ ] partially met   [ ] not met

Plan activities that allow children to explore natural science and the outdoor environment.
[ ] met   [ ] partially met   [ ] not met

MODULE 5: COGNITIVE (continued)

The Competent Staff Member Will:

Provide opportunities for children to participate in and learn about the real world.

[ ] met   [ ] partially met   [ ] not met

Follow a schedule that allows children to choose what they want to do and provides enough time for long-term projects.

[ ] met   [ ] partially met   [ ] not met

Involve children in setting rules and establishing procedures for the program's operations.

[ ] met   [ ] partially met   [ ] not met

Allow children plenty of time to talk to each other and to the staff.

[ ] met   [ ] partially met   [ ] not met

Provide opportunities for children to demonstrate their growing cognitive skills and apply them to new situations.

[ ] met   [ ] partially met   [ ] not met

Introduce children to the steps in problem solving.

[ ] met   [ ] partially met   [ ] not met

Provide opportunities for children to learn in ways that match their learning styles.

[ ] met   [ ] partially met   [ ] not met

MODULE 6: COMMUNICATION

Staff Member: _____

Date/time: _____

Observation Record: _____

Observer: _____

Setting: _____

MODULE 6: COMMUNICATION (continued)

MODULE 6: COMMUNICATION (continued)

Review your records from this observation and others conducted in the last month; score each criterion of competence that you can substantiate.

The Competent Staff Member Will:

Arrange the environment so there are places where children can work, play, and talk in small groups.
[ ] met   [ ] partially met   [ ] not met

Provide materials, time, and space for children to make up their own games and activities.
[ ] met   [ ] partially met   [ ] not met

Provide props, costumes, and other materials that encourage language development activities such as dramatic play, making up skits, and puppetry.
[ ] met   [ ] partially met   [ ] not met

Stock the quiet area with materials that encourage writing—such as pens, pencils, paper, book-binding materials, and a computer, if available.
[ ] met   [ ] partially met   [ ] not met

Include reading and writing materials in all interest areas.
[ ] met   [ ] partially met   [ ] not met

Provide (or arrange for use of) audio and video tape equipment so children can record their storytelling, plays, skits, and other creations.
[ ] met   [ ] partially met   [ ] not met

Include books, magazines, and reference materials in the quiet area in response to children's interests and to expose them to new ideas and topics.
[ ] met   [ ] partially met   [ ] not met

Designate the quiet area as a place where children can do homework.
[ ] met   [ ] partially met   [ ] not met

Respond to children's requests for assistance.
[ ] met   [ ] partially met   [ ] not met

Use printing rather than cursive writing on signs, bulletin boards, and other written materials directed at children.
[ ] met   [ ] partially met   [ ] not met

Ask open-ended questions to encourage children to think and express their ideas.
[ ] met   [ ] partially met   [ ] not met

Accept children's use of slang and popular expressions while serving as a model for standard use of language.
[ ] met   [ ] partially met   [ ] not met

Supporting children's bilingualism through activities and interactions in the program.
[ ] met   [ ] partially met   [ ] not met

Remind children to review the rules before beginning a game or sport so all players can agree on how to play and keep score.
[ ] met   [ ] partially met   [ ] not met

Show respect for what children have to say.
[ ] met   [ ] partially met   [ ] not met

Observe children's nonverbal cues and use the cues to ask questions about their ideas and feelings.
[ ] met   [ ] partially met   [ ] not met

Encourage children to read and write for pleasure, not only because they must complete assigned work.
[ ] met   [ ] partially met   [ ] not met

Help children find the words to express their ideas and feelings.
[ ] met   [ ] partially met   [ ] not met

Use group meetings as opportunities for children to share their ideas, raise concerns, and discuss solutions.
[ ] met   [ ] partially met   [ ] not met

MODULE 6: COMMUNICATION (continued)

The Competent Staff Member Will:

Encourage children to share folklore, oral traditions, stories, songs, and books that reflect their family backgrounds.

[ ] met   [ ] partially met   [ ] not met

Help children plan and implement special interest clubs that use or explore communication skills.

[ ] met   [ ] partially met   [ ] not met

Offer materials and activities that respond to children's individual and developmental skills and interests.

[ ] met   [ ] partially met   [ ] not met

Keep in touch with the elementary schools attended by children to find out what materials and activities the program could offer to build on or enrich the experiences offered in school.

[ ] met   [ ] partially met   [ ] not met

Plan trips and special activities to expand children's language skills and interests.

[ ] met   [ ] partially met   [ ] not met

Build opportunities for children to develop and use communication skills into all program activities, not just those specifically related to reading, writing, listening, and speaking.

[ ] met   [ ] partially met   [ ] not met

MODULE 7: CREATIVE

Staff Member: _____ Observer: _____

Date/time: _____ Setting: _____

Observation Record: _____

MODULE 7: CREATIVE (continued)

MODULE 7: CREATIVE (continued)

Review your records from this observation and others conducted in the last month; score each criterion of competence that you can substantiate.

The Competent Staff Member Will:

Provide open-ended materials with which children can do many things.
[ ] met　　[ ] partially met　　[ ] not met

Arrange the environment so children can spread out, explore, and be messy.
[ ] met　　[ ] partially met　　[ ] not met

Provide sufficient storage space for projects and creations that cannot be completed in one day.
[ ] met　　[ ] partially met　　[ ] not met

Allow creations to stay in place for several days so children can continue using them and possibly expand them.
[ ] met　　[ ] partially met　　[ ] not met

Follow a daily schedule that includes long blocks of time when children are free to organize their own games and activities without adult involvement.
[ ] met　　[ ] partially met　　[ ] not met

Provide sufficient time in the daily schedule for children to make plans and carry them out.
[ ] met　　[ ] partially met　　[ ] not met

Surround children with examples of creative work.
[ ] met　　[ ] partially met　　[ ] not met

Store materials and equipment where children can easily select, replace, and care for them without adult assistance.
[ ] met　　[ ] partially met　　[ ] not met

Offer materials that allow children to explore subjects and interests introduced at school or through experiences such as field trips.
[ ] met　　[ ] partially met　　[ ] not met

Encourage children to express their ideas and feelings.
[ ] met　　[ ] partially met　　[ ] not met

Offer activities that allow children to develop and carry out their own plans.
[ ] met　　[ ] partially met　　[ ] not met

Extend younger children's dramatic play.
[ ] met　　[ ] partially met　　[ ] not met

Introduce children to brainstorming so they can use it as a problem-solving tool.
[ ] met　　[ ] partially met　　[ ] not met

Plan a variety of activities that introduce children to the visual and expressive arts.
[ ] met　　[ ] partially met　　[ ] not met

Help children develop specific skills they can use in their creative work.
[ ] met　　[ ] partially met　　[ ] not met

Respond to children's ideas for projects and activities.
[ ] met　　[ ] partially met　　[ ] not met

Avoid using coloring books, pre-packaged craft projects, and dittos.
[ ] met　　[ ] partially met　　[ ] not met

Value the characteristics that make each child a unique individual.
[ ] met　　[ ] partially met　　[ ] not met

MODULE 7: CREATIVE (continued)

The Competent Staff Member Will:

Help children understand that it takes hard work and practice to develop their talents.
[ ] met   [ ] partially met   [ ] not met

Encourage children to take risks, learn from their mistakes, and try again.
[ ] met   [ ] partially met   [ ] not met

Invite children to display or share the results of their creative work.
[ ] met   [ ] partially met   [ ] not met

Call attention to sensory experiences.
[ ] met   [ ] partially met   [ ] not met

Ask a variety of questions that encourage children to think about things in new ways.
[ ] met   [ ] partially met   [ ] not met

Accept and value each child's unique creative expression.
[ ] met   [ ] partially met   [ ] not met

Model creativity by sharing personal interests, taking risks, and solving problems.
[ ] met   [ ] partially met   [ ] not met

MODULE 8: SELF

Staff Member: _____ **Observer:** _____

Date/time: _____ **Setting:** _____

Observation Record:

MODULE 8: SELF (continued)

MODULE 8: SELF (continued)

Review your records from this observation and others conducted in the last month; score each criterion of competence that you can substantiate.

The Competent Staff Member Will:

Observe children to identify what makes them unique and to let them know their individuality is valued.
[ ] met   [ ] partially met   [ ] not met

Listen carefully to children and take their concerns seriously without interrupting, judging, or giving unasked-for advice.
[ ] met   [ ] partially met   [ ] not met

Show children in many ways they are enjoyable to be with.
[ ] met   [ ] partially met   [ ] not met

Let children know they are cared for by offering gentle physical or nonverbal contact—a hug, a touch, a smile.
[ ] met   [ ] partially met   [ ] not met

Identify children's interests through observation, surveys, and conversations; use the information to plan activities and provide materials.
[ ] met   [ ] partially met   [ ] not met

Know what each child is able to do and show that each child's unique skills and characteristics are valued.
[ ] met   [ ] partially met   [ ] not met

Offer a wide variety of activities that do not limit children's options because of individual differences; make no biased remarks.
[ ] met   [ ] partially met   [ ] not met

Learn words in the native language of children whose first language is not English.
[ ] met   [ ] partially met   [ ] not met

Work with parents and colleagues to make sure each child receives the individual attention he or she needs.
[ ] met   [ ] partially met   [ ] not met

Make sure the program's environment and activities help children learn about and appreciate a variety of cultures and ethnic groups.
[ ] met   [ ] partially met   [ ] not met

Acknowledge children's efforts and accomplishments.
[ ] met   [ ] partially met   [ ] not met

Encourage children to take pride in their efforts and accomplishments.
[ ] met   [ ] partially met   [ ] not met

Reinforce behavior when it is cooperative, helpful, and shows value for other's accomplishments.
[ ] met   [ ] partially met   [ ] not met

Offer sports and games that help children learn to value fairness, cooperation, and personal growth.
[ ] met   [ ] partially met   [ ] not met

Provide opportunities for children to develop leadership skills.
[ ] met   [ ] partially met   [ ] not met

Help children deal with setbacks by accepting their feelings and failures and responding respectfully.
[ ] met   [ ] partially met   [ ] not met

Encourage children to solve their own problems; intervene only when it seems they can't find a solution or when someone might get hurt.
[ ] met   [ ] partially met   [ ] not met

Show children he or she has a positive relationship with their parents and that their family's involvement is both valued and appreciated.
[ ] met   [ ] partially met   [ ] not met

MODULE 8: SELF (continued)

The Competent Staff Member Will:

Encourage children to learn through trial and error.
[ ] met   [ ] partially met   [ ] not met

Involve children in the program's daily operations and weekly chores.
[ ] met   [ ] partially met   [ ] not met

Provide a variety of materials, equipment, and activities to meet a wide range of abilities.
[ ] met   [ ] partially met   [ ] not met

Allow children to use their growing independence in safe and age-appropriate ways.
[ ] met   [ ] partially met   [ ] not met

Provide children with time and resources needed to pursue their interests or to master a skill.
[ ] met   [ ] partially met   [ ] not met

Allow children to choose what they want to do and to choose not to participate in an activity.
[ ] met   [ ] partially met   [ ] not met

Help children gain the skills they need to complete a task so they can overcome fear of failure.
[ ] met   [ ] partially met   [ ] not met

MODULE 9: SOCIAL

Staff Member: _____

Date/time: _____

Observation Record: _____

Observer: _____

Setting: _____

Page 1

MODULE 9: SOCIAL (continued)

MODULE 9: SOCIAL (continued)

Review your records from this observation and others conducted in the last month; score each criterion of competence that you can substantiate.

The Competent Staff Member Will:

Observe and listen to learn how each child relates to the others in the program.
[ ] met   [ ] partially met   [ ] not met

Encourage children to help each other.
[ ] met   [ ] partially met   [ ] not met

Encourage children to solve their own conflicts.
[ ] met   [ ] partially met   [ ] not met

Observe and assist children who have difficulty being accepted by their peers.
[ ] met   [ ] partially met   [ ] not met

Provide enough time in the schedule for self-selected activities so children can decide with whom they would like to be.
[ ] met   [ ] partially met   [ ] not met

Accept children's need to establish their own identities as they use slang and create a "culture" separate from adults.
[ ] met   [ ] partially met   [ ] not met

Identify personal feelings when appropriate to model acceptable ways to express feelings.
[ ] met   [ ] partially met   [ ] not met

Accept children's feelings while helping them learn to control their actions.
[ ] met   [ ] partially met   [ ] not met

Encourage children to value what makes each person a unique individual.
[ ] met   [ ] partially met   [ ] not met

Use group meetings to solve problems that involve all the children.
[ ] met   [ ] partially met   [ ] not met

Model positive ways to interact with other people of all ages.
[ ] met   [ ] partially met   [ ] not met

Plan multi-age activities that encourage cooperation and allow older children to play the role of leader and mentor.
[ ] met   [ ] partially met   [ ] not met

Involve children in establishing rules that encourage use of social skills.
[ ] met   [ ] partially met   [ ] not met

Provide a variety of objects and tools that encourage children to explore their world.
[ ] met   [ ] partially met   [ ] not met

Provide books that help children deal with their feelings about friendship, conflicts, ethnic diversity, and similar topics.
[ ] met   [ ] partially met   [ ] not met

Provide opportunities for children to belong to groups.
[ ] met   [ ] partially met   [ ] not met

Offer opportunities for children to be involved in the community.
[ ] met   [ ] partially met   [ ] not met

Invite community members to share their special knowledge and skills with the children.
[ ] met   [ ] partially met   [ ] not met

MODULE 10: GUIDANCE

Page 1

Staff Member: _____   Observer: _____

Date/time: _____   Setting: _____

Observation Record: _____

_____

_____

_____

_____

_____

_____

_____

_____

_____

_____

_____

_____

_____

_____

_____

MODULE 10: GUIDANCE (continued)

MODULE 10: GUIDANCE (continued)

Prior to the observation period, assess the following criteria.

The Competent Staff Member Will:

Follow a daily schedule that allows children to choose their own activities.
[ ] met [ ] partially met [ ] not met

Make sure there are no safety hazards in the environment.
[ ] met [ ] partially met [ ] not met

Store materials and equipment within children's reach.
[ ] met [ ] partially met [ ] not met

Arrange the environment to encourage appropriate behavior.
[ ] met [ ] partially met [ ] not met

Review your records from this observation and others conducted in the last month; score each criterion of competence that you can substantiate.

The Competent Staff Member Will:

Involve children in setting limits and making rules.
[ ] met [ ] partially met [ ] not met

Involve children in planning activities and selecting materials and equipment.
[ ] met [ ] partially met [ ] not met

Plan some games and activities that encourage cooperation rather than competition.
[ ] met [ ] partially met [ ] not met

Speak to children with the same tone and respect used with adults.
[ ] met [ ] partially met [ ] not met

Consider the possible reasons for the child's behavior.
[ ] met [ ] partially met [ ] not met

Redirect children from inappropriate to appropriate activities.
[ ] met [ ] partially met [ ] not met

Give children opportunities to handle their disagreements without adult assistance.
[ ] met [ ] partially met [ ] not met

State directions and remind children of rules in positive terms.
[ ] met [ ] partially met [ ] not met

Give genuine praise when children use appropriate behavior.
[ ] met [ ] partially met [ ] not met

Discuss children's misbehavior in private conversations.
[ ] met [ ] partially met [ ] not met

Allow children to experience the natural and logical consequences of their behavior.
[ ] met [ ] partially met [ ] not met

Offer assistance to children who are out of control.
[ ] met [ ] partially met [ ] not met

Listen to and accept children's angry feelings while helping them understand the consequences of expressing those feelings inappropriately.
[ ] met [ ] partially met [ ] not met

Talk to children about their day at school, their friends, their concerns, and their feelings.
[ ] met [ ] partially met [ ] not met

Hold group meetings during which children can raise concerns and grievances and work together to solve problems.
[ ] met [ ] partially met [ ] not met

MODULE 10: GUIDANCE (continued)

The Competent Staff Member Will:

Model appropriate ways to express negative feelings.
[ ] met   [ ] partially met   [ ] not met

Provide creative outlets for expressing strong feelings.
[ ] met   [ ] partially met   [ ] not met

Work with parents to help a child with a problem express his or her feelings in acceptable ways.
[ ] met   [ ] partially met   [ ] not met

Teach children how to use conflict resolution techniques to resolve their differences.
[ ] met   [ ] partially met   [ ] not met

MODULE 11: FAMILIES*

Staff Member: _____   **Observer:** _____

Date/time: _____   **Setting:** _____

Observation Record: _____

_____

_____

_____

_____

_____

_____

_____

_____

_____

_____

_____

_____

_____

_____

_____

_____

_____

* Conduct this Competency Assessment at drop-off and/or pick-up time. Interview staff member to verify competencies not readily observable.

MODULE 11: FAMILIES (continued)

MODULE 11: FAMILIES (continued)

Prior to the observation period, assess the following criteria.

The Competent Staff Member Will:

Hold parent-staff conferences to share information about each child's progress and to make plans for the future.
[ ] met   [ ] partially met   [ ] not met

Use a variety of communication strategies to inform parents about the program.
[ ] met   [ ] partially met   [ ] not met

Survey parents' needs and interests and provide appropriate workshops and resources.
[ ] met   [ ] partially met   [ ] not met

Offer a variety of ways to participate in the program to accommodate parents' varied schedules, skills, and interests.
[ ] met   [ ] partially met   [ ] not met

Hold regularly scheduled parent meetings and informal family events at times that are convenient for most parents.
[ ] met   [ ] partially met   [ ] not met

Provide an orientation for new parents so they can get to know staff and learn what children do each day.
[ ] met   [ ] partially met   [ ] not met

Provide information on child development to help parents understand what behaviors are typical of school-age children.
[ ] met   [ ] partially met   [ ] not met

Review your records from this observation and others conducted in the last month; score each criterion of competence that you can substantiate.

The Competent Staff Member Will:

Learn the names of all parents and something about them to build trust.
[ ] met   [ ] partially met   [ ] not met

Share personal information with parents to help them get to know him or her.
[ ] met   [ ] partially met   [ ] not met

Share interesting, positive information about children's activities at the program.
[ ] met   [ ] partially met   [ ] not met

Encourage parents to visit the program at any time.
[ ] met   [ ] partially met   [ ] not met

Let parents know their contributions are appreciated.
[ ] met   [ ] partially met   [ ] not met

Suggest ways to coordinate the child's program and home experiences.
[ ] met   [ ] partially met   [ ] not met

Ask parents to share information about their child's interests and use this information to individualize the program.
[ ] met   [ ] partially met   [ ] not met

Respond to parents' questions and concerns.
[ ] met   [ ] partially met   [ ] not met

Give parents information about a younger child's routines—for example, that the child did not eat snack.
[ ] met   [ ] partially met   [ ] not met

MODULE 11: FAMILIES (continued)

The Competent Staff Member Will:

Involve parents in making decisions about their child's activities at the program.
[ ] met   [ ] partially met   [ ] not met

Maintain confidentiality about all children and families.
[ ] met   [ ] partially met   [ ] not met

Work with parents to help them develop their own strategies for handling a difficult behavior.
[ ] met   [ ] partially met   [ ] not met

Introduce parents to others who live in the same neighborhood or have children of similar ages.
[ ] met   [ ] partially met   [ ] not met

Make an effort to get to know all the parents in the program.
[ ] met   [ ] partially met   [ ] not met

Recognize when parents are under stress and offer additional support.
[ ] met   [ ] partially met   [ ] not met

Notify a supervisor when it seems that parents need professional help.
[ ] met   [ ] partially met   [ ] not met

MODULE 12: PROGRAM MANAGEMENT

Staff Member: _____   Observer: _____

Date/time: _____   Setting: _____

Observation Record: _____

_____

_____

_____

_____

_____

_____

_____

_____

_____

_____

_____

_____

_____

_____

_____

_____

_____

MODULE 12: PROGRAM MANAGEMENT (continued)

MODULE 12: PROGRAM MANAGEMENT (continued)

Review your records from this observation and others conducted in the last month; score each criterion of competence that you can substantiate.

The Competent Staff Member Will:

Use systematic, objective observation to accurately record what children say and do.

[ ] met   [ ] partially met   [ ] not met

Observe children in different settings and at different times of the day.

[ ] met   [ ] partially met   [ ] not met

Conduct observations for specific reasons.

[ ] met   [ ] partially met   [ ] not met

Record many instances of a child's actions before drawing conclusions.

[ ] met   [ ] partially met   [ ] not met

Share observation information with parents and encourage them to help their children grow and develop.

[ ] met   [ ] partially met   [ ] not met

Develop an observation schedule with colleagues so every child is observed on a regular basis.

[ ] met   [ ] partially met   [ ] not met

Conduct periodic joint observations to ensure accuracy.

[ ] met   [ ] partially met   [ ] not met

Participate in regular staff meetings to plan and evaluate the program.

[ ] met   [ ] partially met   [ ] not met

Discuss observation recordings with colleagues when planning for individuals and for the group.

[ ] met   [ ] partially met   [ ] not met

Use parent surveys and open-ended questionnaires to collect information about children and to evaluate the program.

[ ] met   [ ] partially met   [ ] not met

Involve children in planning and evaluating the program.

[ ] met   [ ] partially met   [ ] not met

Change aspects of the program to address individual cultures, interests, needs, and abilities.

[ ] met   [ ] partially met   [ ] not met

Conduct periodic surveys to identify children's interests and to encourage them to evaluate the program.

[ ] met   [ ] partially met   [ ] not met

Help children form clubs that allow them to explore their shared interests.

[ ] met   [ ] partially met   [ ] not met

Appreciate and use the strengths of other team members.

[ ] met   [ ] partially met   [ ] not met

Coordinate with appropriate resources in the community.

[ ] met   [ ] partially met   [ ] not met

Use creative thinking skills in planning and problem solving.

[ ] met   [ ] partially met   [ ] not met

Meet and talk with colleagues and the supervisor to provide input on program issues.

[ ] met   [ ] partially met   [ ] not met

Keep informed about job responsibilities and program policies and procedures.

[ ] met   [ ] partially met   [ ] not met

MODULE 12: PROGRAM MANAGEMENT (continued)

The Competent Staff Member Will:

Review program policies before starting a new task.
[ ] met   [ ] partially met   [ ] not met

Complete management tasks according to a schedule.
[ ] met   [ ] partially met   [ ] not met

Follow the program's system for accurate and timely record keeping.
[ ] met   [ ] partially met   [ ] not met

Provide substitute staff with adequate information on weekly plans and program practices.
[ ] met   [ ] partially met   [ ] not met

Answer parents' questions about program policies and procedures; refer parents to the supervisor when appropriate.
[ ] met   [ ] partially met   [ ] not met

Appendix D

Tracking Forms

Individual Tracking Form

Name: _____

Indicate Date Completed

Module	Over-view	Pre-Training Assess-ment	L.A. I	L.A. II	L.A. III	L.A. IV	L.A. V	L.A. VI	Know-ledge Assess-ment	Compe-tency Assess-ment	Trainer Sign-off
Orientation	X	X	X	X	X	X	X	X	X	X	
1. Safe								X			
2. Healthy								X			
3. Program Environment								X			
4. Physical								X			
5. Cognitive								X			
6. Communication								X			
7. Creative								X			
8. Self								X			
9. Social								X			
10. Guidance											
11. Families								X			
12. Program Management								X			
13. Professionalism								X		X	

247

Program Tracking Form

Modules

Staff Members	OR		1		2		3		4		5		6		7		8		9		10		11		12		13	
	B	C	B	C	B	C	B	C	B	C	B	C	B	C	B	C	B	C	B	C	B	C	B	C	B	C

Legend

B - Begun
C - Completed

Modules:

OR - Orientation
1 - Safe
2 - Healthy
3 - Program
     Environment

4 - Physical
5 - Cognitive
6 - Communication
7 - Creative
8 - Self

9 - Social
10 - Guidance
11 - Families
12 - Program Management
13 - Professionalism

Appendix E

Training Record

Training Record

Name: _____

Program: _____

Topic	Date(s)	Hours	Type of Training (conference, course, workshop, observation/feedback)	Agency Providing Training	Signature of Trainer

Appendix F

Certificate of Completion

CERTIFICATE of COMPLETION

AWARDED TO

_____

for completion of _____ hours of training

on *Caring for Children in School-Age Programs*

_____ 199 _____

Verification of Training may be obtained from:

Agency Sponsoring Training: _____

Sponsor's Address: _____

City/State/Zip: _____

Sponsor's Phone Number: (___) _____

_____
(Instructor's Signature)

Appendix G

Publishers and Distributors of Resources

Publishers and Distributors of Resources

In the Orientation to *Caring for Children in School-Age Programs* you will find a list of recommended resources. Publishers and distributors of these resources are listed below.

Addison-Wesley Publishing Company
1 Jacob Way
Reading, MA 01867
617-944-3700
800-447-2226

Andrews and McMeel
4900 Main Street
Kansas City, MO 64112
816-932-6700
800-826-4216

American Public Health Association
1015 Fifteenth Street, NW
Washington, DC 20005
202-789-5600

American Academy of Pediatrics
141 Northwest Point Boulevard
Elk Grove Village, IL 60009

Bantam Books
201 E. 50th Street
New York, NY 10022
212-751-2600

Basic Books
Harper Collins Publishers
10 E. 53rd Street
New York, NY 10022-5299
212-207-7057
800-242-7737

Bright Ring Publishing
P. O. Box 31338
Bellingham, WA 98228
206-734-1601

Centers for Disease Control
1600 Clifton Road, NE
Atlanta, GA 30333
404-639-3311

Center for Early Adolescence
University of North Carolina at Chapel Hill
D-2 Carr Mill Town Center
Carrboro, NC 27510
919-966-1148

Delmar Publishers, Inc.
P. O. Box 15015
Albany, NY 12205-5015
518-464-3500
800-347-7707

Dolphin Books
Doubleday and Company
1540 Broadway
New York, NY 10036-4094
212-782-8200

Early Educators Press
P. O. Box 1177
Lake Alfred, FL 33850
813-956-1569

Exceptional Parent Press
209 Harvard Street, Suite 303
Brookline, MA 02146
617-730-5800

Exchange Press, Inc.
P. O. Box 2890
Redmond, WA 98073
206-883-9394

Fearon Teachers Aids
4350 Equity Drive
Columbus, OH 43228
217-357-3900

The Free Press
866 3rd Avenue
New York, NY 10022
212-702-2000

Free Spirit Publishers
400 First Avenue N., Suite 616
Minneapolis, MN 55401-1730
612-338-2068
800-735-7323

Gryphon House, Inc.
P. O. Box 207
Beltsville, MD 20704-0207
301-595-9500
800-638-0928

Harbinger House
P. O. Box 42948
Tucson, AZ 85733-2948
602-326-9595
800-759-9945

Harper Collins Publishers
1000 Keystone Industrial Park
Scranton, PA 18512
800-331-3761

Houghton-Mifflin
222 Berkeley Street
Boston, MA 02116
617-725-5000
800-225-3362

Little, Brown and Company
1271 Avenue of the Americas
New York, NY 10020
212-522-8700
800-759-0190

McGraw Hill
220 E. Daniel Dale Road
DeSoto, TX 75115
800-442-9685

Meadowbrook Press
18318 Minnetonka Boulevard
Deephaven, MN 55391
612-473-5400
800-338-2232

National Association for the Education of
   Young Children
1509 16th Street, NW
Washington, DC 20036-1426
202-232-8777
800-424-2460

National Association of
   Elementary School Principals
1615 Duke Street
Alexandria, VA 22314-3483
703-684-3345

Pantheon Books
Random House, Inc.
201 E. 50th Street
New York, NY 10022
212-872-8238
800-638-6460

Perigee Books
The Putnam Publishing Group
200 Madison Avenue
New York, NY 10016
212-951-8400

Playground International
P. O. Box 33363
Austin, TX 78764

Play Today Press
P. O. Box 161713
601 Lisa Drive
Austin, TX 78733-2418
512-301-3088

Random House, Inc.
201 E. 50th Street
New York, NY 10022
212-751-2600
800-733-3000

R & E Research Associates
468 Auzerais Avenue, Suite A
San Jose, CA 95126
408-977-0691

Redleaf Press
450 North Syndicate, Suite 5
St. Paul, MN 55104-9951
800-423-8309
612-641-0305

School-Age Child Care Project
Center for Research on Women
Wellesley College
106 Central Street
Wellesley, MA 02181-8259
617-283-2544

School-Age NOTES
P. O. Box 40205
Nashville, TN 37204
615-242-8464

School-Age Workshops Press
P. O. Box 5012
Huntington Beach, CA 92615-5012
714-968-6732

Scott, Foresman, and Company
1900 E. Lake Avenue
Glenview, IL 60025
708-729-3000
800-554-4411

Simon & Schuster
P. O. Box 11071
Des Moines, IA 50336
800-374-1200

Ten Speed Press
P. O. Box 7123
Berkeley, CA 94707
510-845-8414
800-841-2665

Times Books
Random House, Inc.
400 Hahn Road
Westminister, MD 21157
212-751-2600
800-733-3000

U. S. Consumer Products
   Safety Commission
Washington, DC 20207
301-504-0580

William Morrow and Company, Inc.
1350 Avenue of the Americas
New York, NY 10019
212-261-6500

Williamson Publishing
Church Hill Road, P. O. Box 185
Charlotte, VT 05445
802-425-2102
800-234-8791

Workman Publishing Group
708 Broadway
New York, NY 10003
212-254-5900
800-722-7202

NOTES

NOTES

NOTES

NOTES